WELCOME TO WREXHAM: THE RISE OF THE RED DRAGONS

How Ryan Reynolds and Rob McElhenney Transformed the Welsh Football Club

BY

REGINA BRAIDEN

DISCLAIMER

The content in **"Welcome to Wrexham: The Rise of the Red Dragons"** is based on publicly available information, interviews, and sources at the time of writing. While every effort has been made to ensure accuracy, the book is intended for general informational and entertainment purposes.

The author is not directly affiliated with Wrexham AFC, its owners, or any related entities. Any views or opinions expressed are those of the author and do not represent the official positions of Wrexham AFC, Ryan Reynolds, Rob McElhenney, or their teams.

Any trademarks, logos, or intellectual property mentioned are owned by their respective parties and are used for identification and educational purposes.

While this book reflects the author's best efforts to present an accurate account, some details may change over time. The author and publisher do not accept responsibility for any inaccuracies or omissions, and readers are encouraged to verify information as needed.

TABLE OF CONTENTS

CHAPTER 1

ROOTS OF THE RED DRAGONS

Long before Hollywood lights ever gleamed on the Racecourse Ground, Wrexham AFC stood tall as a beacon of Welsh football pride. Founded in 1864, Wrexham Association Football Club is not just one of the oldest football clubs in the world — it's a cultural monument woven deeply into the fabric of a working-class town that breathes the game. Its story is one of resilience, community, heartbreak, and hope — values that shaped it for over 160 years before two actors from across the Atlantic cast their lot with the Red Dragons.

Wrexham, located in North Wales, is a town rich in industrial heritage. The club was born out of a local cricket club's desire to stay fit during the winter. Matches were played on the hallowed turf of the Racecourse Ground, now recognized as the **oldest international stadium still in use** — a ground that has hosted Welsh national team matches since 1877.

In the late 19th and early 20th centuries, Wrexham AFC earned a reputation as a formidable force in Welsh football. The club's golden age included multiple Welsh Cup victories and forays into the English Football League (EFL), where it competed against some of England's most storied teams. The club became a focal point for national pride and a unifying force for the community, often drawing thousands to the Racecourse on matchdays — miners, teachers, laborers, families — all united in red.

One of the club's most iconic moments came in 1992, when **Wrexham, a Fourth Division side, stunned First Division giants Arsenal 2–1 in the FA Cup**. It was a classic underdog tale, a match still talked about today with awe and reverence. The town erupted, and the result resonated far beyond Wales — a testament to the club's spirit and potential.

But the glory days gave way to hardship. The 2000s brought financial troubles and ownership instability. By 2008, Wrexham had been relegated from the Football League for the first time in 87 years, plunging into the fifth tier of English football — the National League. For over a decade, the club languished in relative obscurity, surviving only because of its diehard supporters who refused to let their club die.

In 2011, **Wrexham Supporters Trust**, a fan-led group, took control of the club after a dramatic vote. This marked a new chapter defined by community ownership. The fans weren't just cheering from the stands — they were running the club. It was a unique experiment in modern football, one driven by passion rather than profit.

The trust's stewardship stabilized Wrexham but couldn't reverse years of decline overnight. Promotion back to the Football League proved elusive. Despite spirited attempts and playoff appearances, the club remained stuck in the National League — until 2020, when a strange and unexpected rumor started to spread online: **Two Hollywood actors wanted to buy Wrexham AFC**.

Skepticism quickly turned to curiosity, then excitement. When Ryan Reynolds and Rob McElhenney officially announced their intentions, it wasn't just a potential takeover — it was a lifeline. But before the glamour and cameras, before the docuseries and global fandom, there was a club built by generations of local hands and hearts.

This is where the story begins — not with celebrity, but with tradition. Wrexham AFC's roots run deep. They are the reason the club could be reborn, the reason people cared, and the reason why, when the world finally took notice, there was a foundation strong enough to carry the weight of a dream.

The Hollywood Duo Behind Wrexham's Revival

In the grand theatre of football, stories of club ownership are often painted with familiar strokes. Former legends returning to nurture their boyhood teams, billionaires planting flags in new territories, lifelong fans finally stepping from the stands into the boardroom. But in 2020, the footballing world paused, blinked, and did a double take when the tiny town of Wrexham, nestled in the northeast of Wales, found its unlikely saviors not in football royalty, but on the silver screens of Hollywood.

Welcome to *Wrexham*: The Rise of the Red Dragons

Ryan Reynolds and Rob McElhenney. Two names that, until then, had little to do with the muddy boots and echoing stands of the National League. Known more for blockbuster films and comedy shows than touchline tactics or transfer windows, their interest in Wrexham AFC was met with a cocktail of surprise, skepticism, and, eventually, a hope that hadn't stirred in years.

But this wasn't a publicity stunt. This wasn't a vanity project. This was something else entirely.

It began with curiosity—Rob McElhenney, the creative mind behind *It's Always Sunny in Philadelphia*, found himself falling in love with football's soul. Not the elite spectacle of Champions League finals or World Cup drama, but the gritty beauty of lower-league football. The kind where the grass isn't always perfect, the seats are weathered, and the victories feel like life's greatest moments. He saw in football what many who grew up with it sometimes forget: that this game is not just a sport, but a lifeline.

It was Rob's idea to take this passion one step further. He didn't want to simply watch. He wanted to belong. But to pull it off, he knew he needed a partner with vision, charisma, and—let's be honest—a little bit of star power. So he reached out to a friend whose work ethic matched his heart: Ryan Reynolds.

The pairing was unexpected. Ryan, the global film star with charm as sharp as his comedic timing, had little direct connection to football. But he was a storyteller, and Wrexham's story—its 158-year history, its working-class roots, its years in the football wilderness—was irresistible.

Together, they did what few celebrities dared to even consider. They bought a fifth-tier football club in a country neither of them had ever lived in, playing a sport neither of them had grown up with. And they did it with respect, humility, and one unwavering belief: that Wrexham AFC was more than a club. It was a heartbeat.

Welcome to *Wrexham*: The Rise of the Red Dragons

From the outset, their intentions were clear. This wasn't about turning Wrexham into a reality show or a novelty act. This was about honoring the town's heritage, preserving its footballing spirit, and giving it the tools to dream again. They weren't just here to write checks. They were here to listen, to learn, and to lead with purpose.

Their arrival injected fresh energy into a club that had been weighed down by years of near misses, financial struggles, and fading ambitions. Wrexham fans, known for their loyalty and grit, had endured decades of disappointment. But now, a spark had returned. Not just because of who the owners were—but because of how they made people feel.

Ryan and Rob didn't just speak to fans. They spoke *with* them.

They visited the Racecourse Ground, walked the streets of Wrexham, and sat with supporters who had been there long before any cameras showed up. They met local business owners, charity workers, and lifelong fans who told stories of matches gone by, of family legacies tied to the club, of heartbreaks and heroes. They made it clear: they weren't here to change Wrexham's identity. They were here to amplify it.

And then came the documentary.

FX and Disney+ partnered with the duo to create *Welcome to Wrexham*, a fly-on-the-wall docuseries that chronicled the club's journey under their stewardship. But unlike the glossy, scripted productions of other sporting narratives, this was raw and real. It showed the tension in the locker rooms, the anxiety in the boardroom, the hope in the hearts of fans young and old. It humanized a club long overshadowed by bigger names, and suddenly, the world took notice.

From Philadelphia to Vancouver, new fans were born—not because of celebrity, but because they saw what football could mean to a town like Wrexham. They saw a father and son cry after a dramatic win. They saw players battling for contracts, not millions. They saw a club trying to climb not just a table, but out of a history of hardship.

Reynolds and McElhenney had cracked something powerful: a reminder that football's most beautiful stories aren't always found at the top. Sometimes, they rise from the muddiest corners of the pyramid, carried by people who simply care.

Of course, they weren't perfect. Mistakes were made. There were awkward learning curves—mispronounced names, misunderstood rules, moments where their American optimism clashed with British realism. But they embraced it all. They laughed at themselves, owned their errors, and kept moving forward.

Most importantly, they backed their vision with action.

They invested in the infrastructure—upgrading facilities, improving training resources, and working closely with the local council to regenerate the club's surroundings. They put people in positions of trust, hiring experienced football minds to ensure decisions were made with wisdom, not impulse. And they showed faith in manager Phil Parkinson, giving him the time and support needed to build something sustainable.

Results followed.

Wrexham's squad grew stronger. The style of play became bolder. The Racecourse buzzed with an energy not felt in decades. And through it all, the fans came in droves—both the lifelong diehards and the new followers from around the globe, united by the story unfolding in this proud Welsh town.

But for Ryan and Rob, the truest measure of success wasn't just promotion or profit. It was the moments that couldn't be scripted.

Welcome to *Wrexham*: The Rise of the Red Dragons

Like when they met a 100-year-old fan who'd attended matches since the 1930s. Or when they saw a packed crowd welcome the team home after a crucial away win. Or when local children proudly wore Wrexham kits with their heads held high, not because of fame, but because they finally had heroes to believe in again.

This wasn't just ownership. It was stewardship.

They had taken on more than a club. They had taken on a community. And they embraced that responsibility with the same passion they'd brought to their creative careers. They understood that football wasn't just about goals. It was about identity, memory, and belonging.

In a world where many clubs are treated like assets—bought, sold, flipped, forgotten—Wrexham found owners who saw something deeper. Who saw the magic in a club that had been overlooked for too long. Who saw the humanity in the game, and the heartbeat in the stands.

And so, as Wrexham marches forward, dreams bigger, and continues its rise through the leagues, the story of Ryan Reynolds and Rob McElhenney will remain a defining chapter. Not because they were famous. But because they cared.

They reminded the footballing world that even in an era of superclubs and satellite deals, there is still room for romance. For miracles. For two men from Hollywood to fall in love with a club from North Wales—and help it believe in itself once more.

Ryan Reynolds: From Vancouver to Global Stardom

Before he ever set foot on the hallowed pitch of the Racecourse Ground, Ryan Reynolds had already played countless roles— romantic leads, comic book heroes, deadpan narrators, and real-life entrepreneur. But the journey that would one day lead him to the town of Wrexham, to co-own one of the oldest football clubs in the world, began thousands of miles away from Wales—in the quiet neighborhoods of Vancouver, British Columbia.

Born on October 23, 1976, Ryan Rodney Reynolds was the youngest of four boys in an Irish Catholic household. His father, James Chester Reynolds, was a food wholesaler—a tough, disciplined man who instilled in his children the value of hard work and grit. His mother, Tamara Lee Stewart, a retail salesperson, provided the emotional warmth and grounded perspective that would balance out the household. Life in Vancouver was ordinary, modest, and far removed from the limelight that would one day define Ryan's existence.

From a young age, Reynolds showed a spark. It wasn't just about being funny or charming—though he was both in spades—it was his ability to adapt, to shift tones, and to connect with people that set him apart. At just 13, he landed his first acting role on *Hillside* (also known as *Fifteen* in the U.S.), a Canadian teen soap opera that gave him his first taste of fame. It wasn't glamourous—filming was relentless, the scripts cheesy—but it lit a fire. The camera, it seemed, loved him. And Reynolds, in turn, fell in love with the possibilities.

His early career in Hollywood was a slow burn. There were lean years—auditions that led nowhere, scripts that didn't quite land, and roles that paid the bills but didn't excite the soul. For a time, Reynolds considered giving up acting altogether. But every time he thought of walking away, something pulled him back in. Maybe it was the support of his family, maybe the inner drive, or perhaps the idea that his story wasn't finished yet.

Then came *Two Guys and a Girl* (1998–2001), a sitcom that didn't just give him steady work—it gave him a platform. As Michael "Berg" Bergen, Reynolds displayed a now-familiar blend of sarcasm, quick wit, and warmth. It was a role that hinted at his potential, a stepping stone toward something bigger.

Over the years, Reynolds slowly carved out a niche. He wasn't just the funny guy; he had range. Romantic comedies like *Definitely, Maybe* and *The Proposal* showed his emotional depth, while thrillers like *Buried* revealed a more serious, dramatic side. Still, Hollywood, ever fickle, had not fully embraced him as a true leading man.

That all changed—with a bump and then a bang.

In 2011, Reynolds took on the titular role in *Green Lantern*, a superhero film that was meant to elevate him to blockbuster status. Instead, it flopped. Critics were brutal, box office returns underwhelming, and the experience left Reynolds disillusioned. He later referred to the film as a misstep, but it would prove to be a pivotal moment. Failure, he discovered, wasn't the end. It was fuel.

It was *Deadpool* (2016) that redefined his career—and, in many ways, his life. The wisecracking, fourth-wall-breaking antihero was everything Hollywood had tried to suppress: irreverent, raunchy, unpredictable, and utterly human. Reynolds fought for years to get the project made, even leaking test footage online to build fan demand. And when it finally hit theaters, it exploded. Audiences loved it. Critics praised it. And Reynolds? He wasn't just back—he was unstoppable.

Yet fame was never enough. Beneath the sarcasm and star power was a man with vision. Reynolds wasn't content to be just another actor collecting roles. He wanted to shape narratives—both on screen and off.

In 2018, he co-founded **Maximum Effort**, a production company and marketing firm that quickly became known for its bold, unconventional advertising style. Whether promoting films, brands, or causes, Reynolds' voice—authentic, cheeky, and always clever—stood out in an industry often drowning in noise.

But it wasn't just about making noise. It was about making impact.

Reynolds began to branch out into business. His investment in **Aviation Gin**, once a quiet name in the spirits industry, turned into a branding masterclass. With Maximum Effort's marketing behind it—and Reynolds as the face—the company soared, eventually selling to Diageo for a deal reportedly worth over $600 million. He bought a stake in **Mint Mobile**, a discount wireless provider, bringing his marketing genius to a field that few actors would ever dare touch. He invested in **Wealthsimple**, a Canadian financial tech company, and in **1Password**, a cybersecurity firm. Every move wasn't just strategic—it was personal.

Ryan Reynolds had become more than a Hollywood actor. He had become a cultural force.

And then—Wrexham.

When Rob McElhenney approached him about buying a football club in Wales, it might have sounded like a punchline. But Reynolds, ever curious and ever daring, didn't laugh. He leaned in. What began as a conversation about possibility quickly turned into purpose. It wasn't about owning a club—it was about being part of something real. Something enduring.

Ryan didn't grow up watching football. But he understood what it meant to people. He understood what it meant to belong to something bigger than yourself. And he understood storytelling— Wrexham, with its rich history and struggling present, was a story worth telling.

Reynolds brought more than money to the table. He brought energy, empathy, and respect. He made an effort to learn—about the game, the town, the fans. He met players and staff not as a distant owner, but as an invested partner. He spoke to fans not as a celebrity, but as a custodian of their beloved club. In press conferences and interviews, he always turned the spotlight back to Wrexham, back to the community.

And when the cameras of *Welcome to Wrexham* rolled, they captured not just his charm but his sincerity. Fans across the world were introduced to a side of Ryan Reynolds that few had seen before—one not defined by red carpets, but by red shirts and roaring chants.

In one episode, Reynolds sits quietly in the Racecourse Ground, watching the team battle it out. His eyes are fixed, his expression tense. It's not acting. It's passion. He has become what so many fans already are—emotionally tethered to the fate of a club that defines a town.

For Wrexham supporters, this connection mattered more than box office numbers. Here was an owner who showed up. Who cared. Who felt.

In a world where fame is often fleeting, and celebrity interest in sports can be shallow or short-lived, Ryan Reynolds has proven to be different. His involvement with Wrexham isn't a hobby—it's a legacy in the making.

He once said, "I believe that businesses can be personal. That brands can have heart." His journey with Wrexham AFC is a living example. Because in this story, Ryan Reynolds isn't just a movie star. He's a Red Dragon.

From Vancouver to Wrexham, from early sitcoms to football stadiums, the arc of Ryan Reynolds' career is far from conventional. But it's exactly this unpredictability—this willingness to take risks, to invest in people, to find meaning in unlikely places—that makes his chapter in the Wrexham story so compelling.

And for the fans, that makes all the difference.

From Philly to the Pitch – Rob McElhenney's Creative Heart and Footballing Soul

Long before the floodlights of the Racecourse Ground lit his path, before chants of "Wrexham! Wrexham!" echoed with his name entwined, Robert Dale McElhenney was just a kid from South Philly with a wild imagination and a restless spirit. His story is not just about acting, writing, or owning a football club—it's about reinvention, resilience, and relentless belief in storytelling that connects deeply with the human condition.

Born on April 14, 1977, in Philadelphia, Pennsylvania, Rob's upbringing was anything but glitzy. Raised in a traditional Roman Catholic household, his early years were deeply influenced by the vibrant, gritty energy of his hometown—a city where sports are religion, loyalty is currency, and every win or loss is felt like a communal heartbeat. That sense of identity would later become a compass for his career—and eventually, his venture into football.

Rob didn't grow up in the spotlight, but the seeds of performance and observation were planted early. His parents divorced when he was just eight years old, a turning point that added emotional texture to his worldview. He later described his family as "a little off," but full of love. That blend of dysfunction and affection would become the creative DNA of his most iconic work.

After a few minor acting gigs in the late '90s and early 2000s, McElhenney did what many struggling creatives do—he took matters into his own hands. Armed with a micro-budget, two close friends, and an unapologetic creative vision, he created *It's Always Sunny in Philadelphia* in 2005. At the time, few could have predicted the seismic shift this scrappy sitcom would trigger in American television.

Sunny was not a safe show. It didn't pander to audiences or polish its characters for mass appeal. Instead, it handed viewers a crew of morally bankrupt bar owners—The Gang—who stumbled through life with wild selfishness, ignorance, and a shocking absence of growth. And yet, it worked. Brilliantly.

McElhenney played Ronald "Mac" McDonald, a character whose journey from wannabe tough guy to self-accepting gay man was both riotous and surprisingly moving. Rob's portrayal was layered—often absurd but never lacking in sincerity. He wrote. He directed. He took wild risks. He once gained over 60 pounds for a season, just to parody how sitcom characters inexplicably become better-looking over time. Then, a few seasons later, he transformed his body into that of a shredded action star—without any studio demand—just to subvert expectations again.

This wasn't just commitment to comedy; it was a commitment to truth through absurdity.

Behind the camera, Rob was a builder. He helped shape *Sunny* into one of the longest-running live-action sitcoms in TV history, a show that didn't just entertain but challenged. Social taboos, politics, race, sexuality—nothing was off-limits. And perhaps most importantly, he proved that authenticity, however twisted, can resonate far deeper than formulas ever could.

But McElhenney wasn't content to be a one-show man.

In 2020, he co-created *Mythic Quest: Raven's Banquet*, a sharp and soulful workplace comedy for Apple TV+. The show followed a fictional video game development studio—hardly traditional sitcom fare. But Rob, once again, infused it with unexpected humanity. His character, Ian Grimm, was a genius game creator with a god complex and a fragile ego. Think Steve Jobs meets Deadpool, only slightly more emotionally available.

Mythic Quest was funny, sure. But what made it remarkable was its emotional resonance. The show tackled grief, ambition, identity, and generational dynamics with the kind of sensitivity one wouldn't expect from the man who once played Mac. It proved Rob had grown—not just as an artist, but as a storyteller.

Still, for all his Hollywood success, McElhenney never lost sight of his working-class roots. He understood community. He understood struggle. He knew what it meant to fight for something that mattered—something bigger than yourself.

Which brings us to Wrexham.

When the opportunity came to invest in a football club, most might have expected McElhenney to pick something glossier. A Premier League team. A franchise in Los Angeles. Something with instant return. But that wasn't the story he wanted to tell. He wanted grit. He wanted history. He wanted heart.

And he found it in Wrexham AFC.

The club, founded in 1864, was a sleeping giant—rich in tradition, starved of glory. The town, nestled in North Wales, was fiercely loyal but had weathered tough economic storms. It was a place of resilience, of community pride—and Rob fell in love with it.

But there was a catch. He needed money. A lot of it.

That's when he called Ryan Reynolds.

The two had only communicated via social media prior, but McElhenney had a vision and knew Reynolds had the charisma, reach, and passion to match. Over a Zoom call, Rob pitched more than a business proposal—he pitched a dream. A real-life redemption arc. A football fairytale. And Reynolds, to his eternal credit, said yes.

Together, they formed RR McReynolds Company LLC and acquired Wrexham AFC in November 2020. But it wasn't just a purchase. It was a partnership—with each other, with the town, and with the global football community.

Welcome to *Wrexham*: The Rise of the Red Dragons

From the start, Rob approached the club not as a celebrity, but as a steward. He learned the rules. He studied the history. He immersed himself in the culture of football and the culture of Wales. He walked the streets of Wrexham, listened to the fans, visited the pubs, and respected the club's heartbeat.

And he brought his storytelling magic.

Welcome to Wrexham, the docuseries produced for FX and Disney+, wasn't just a behind-the-scenes look at a football takeover. It was a human drama—part sport, part spirit. The show introduced global audiences to the people of Wrexham: the groundskeepers, the lifelong supporters, the single moms, the injured players, and the pub landlords. McElhenney wasn't just filming a documentary—he was building empathy, rewriting the script of what club ownership could look like.

In one of the most moving episodes, Rob opens up about his own journey with dyslexia and learning difficulties. He talks about fatherhood, about vulnerability, about being a better man. The scene resonated not because it was polished—but because it was real.

For the people of Wrexham, this sincerity mattered. They had seen clubs mismanaged. They had seen rich owners disappear. But here were two men—not from Wales, not even from the UK—who showed up, who stayed, and who listened.

Rob once said, "I don't want to just make TV shows—I want to make people feel seen." With Wrexham AFC, he's done exactly that.

He didn't just bring funding to the club—he brought visibility, excitement, and hope. He supported player development, improved the stadium, and revived a culture of belief. And as results improved and promotion hopes climbed, so too did the global recognition of Wrexham as more than a football club. It became a symbol of what can happen when stories are told with heart.

Welcome to *Wrexham*: The Rise of the Red Dragons

For football fans, especially those who've followed lower-league teams through thick and thin, Rob's story is a beacon. He's not the billionaire tycoon with no ties to the sport. He's the passionate fan who did his homework. The storyteller who chose the underdog. The showrunner who made the pitch his new stage.

And as the stands fill up at the Racecourse, as chants rise into the chilly Welsh air, one thing becomes clear: Rob McElhenney didn't just buy a club—he joined a family.

A Shared Vision – Reviving Wrexham AFC

Every great story starts with a dream. But the tale of Wrexham AFC's revival began with something more profound—a shared belief in the power of people, place, and purpose.

When Rob McElhenney first imagined owning a football club, he was a man with no formal ties to the sport, no business in European football, and no roadmap for navigating the world of lower-league clubs. But what he *did* have was vision. A storyteller at heart, Rob saw something universal in Wrexham—a town steeped in history, passionate about its club, and yearning for a return to glory.

But he also knew he couldn't do it alone.

Enter Ryan Reynolds—Hollywood star, global icon, and as it turns out, a kindred spirit. Their friendship had begun in the most 21st-century way possible: over Twitter. Casual online banter turned into private messages, which quickly evolved into long conversations about storytelling, legacy, and… football.

Rob didn't approach Ryan with a business pitch. He came with a narrative. A real-life underdog story. A club with 150+ years of history, a loyal fanbase, and the oldest international stadium still in use. He painted the picture: two outsiders, coming together not to chase profit, but to restore pride—to lift a community by lifting its beloved club.

Ryan, for his part, didn't laugh it off. He leaned in. He saw what Rob saw. And he felt the weight of the opportunity.

Their joint vision crystallized quickly. In 2020, they formally announced their intention to purchase Wrexham AFC. But they didn't waltz in with wallets waving. Instead, they submitted themselves to the very fans whose hearts they hoped to win.

The Wrexham Supporters Trust (WST)—a group of local fans who had owned and sustained the club for nearly a decade—held the keys. This wasn't a buyout. It was a handover. A sacred passing of the torch.

Reynolds and McElhenney could have made the process private. But instead, they went public—transparent from the start. They released heartfelt videos explaining their motivations, promising to listen, to learn, and to lead with humility. They pledged not just financial investment but emotional commitment. They vowed to protect the club's identity while ushering in a new era of possibility.

In November 2020, the fans voted. Over **98%** of WST members approved the sale. It was an overwhelming, emotional endorsement—and in February 2021, the takeover became official.

From that moment on, Wrexham AFC was no longer just a football club. It was a lightning rod for hope.

Their approach was methodical, respectful, and bold. First came investments in the club's infrastructure. The historic Racecourse Ground, a sacred site for Welsh football, began undergoing revitalization. Plans were laid for a new stand, improved facilities, and upgrades that would serve fans and players alike.

Then came the footballing side. Executive roles were filled with seasoned professionals. Player recruitment was ramped up, and the budget—once painfully modest—was now competitive. But the goal wasn't to throw money blindly. Rob and Ryan wanted smart growth. Sustainable success. Wins that would mean something.

Off the pitch, they doubled down on community. Charitable efforts expanded. Local businesses were promoted. Wrexham's brand started appearing on international stages—in interviews, on social media, and on television screens from Los Angeles to Lagos. But always with one rule: the focus stayed on the people of Wrexham.

This philosophy reached its most powerful form in *Welcome to Wrexham*, a documentary series unlike any other. Part sports doc, part social chronicle, part comedy, the show peeled back the layers—not just of a football club, but of a town and its spirit.

Viewers met real fans like Millie, a teenage girl with cerebral palsy whose passion for Wrexham was contagious. They met Jordan Davies, a young player whose heartbreak off the field mirrored the drama on it. They followed lifelong supporters, ground staff, volunteers, and pub regulars—people whose lives were inextricably linked to the badge.

And through it all, Rob and Ryan weren't actors playing owners. They were *in it*. Traveling back and forth. Sitting nervously in the stands. Crying at losses. Celebrating promotions. Grieving with players. Laughing with locals. Learning Welsh phrases. Toasting strangers. Falling in love with Wrexham just like Wrexham fell in love with them.

It was never perfect. The early months were rocky. Expectations were high. The team stumbled. The media watched closely. Critics whispered. But the ownership duo never blinked. They owned the setbacks. They communicated clearly. And they doubled down on the mission.

By the 2022–23 season, the dream started to take shape. Under manager Phil Parkinson, the team surged. Matches were electric. The fans roared louder. A 3-2 FA Cup thriller against Sheffield United reminded the world what magic football can still conjure. And then, on a night etched forever into club lore, **Wrexham won promotion to League Two**, ending a **15-year exile from the Football League**.

Tears flowed freely—from players, from fans, from Rob and Ryan themselves.

For a club that had seen so much heartbreak, this was more than a victory. It was vindication. It was healing. It was rebirth.

But most of all, it was proof.

Proof that football, at its best, isn't about balance sheets or branding. It's about belief. About relationships. About showing up, season after season, even when the odds are stacked against you.

Ryan and Rob didn't just show up—they stayed. They built something lasting. They didn't strip the club for parts. They gave it new breath.

Their story with Wrexham is still being written. There are more promotions to chase. More stands to rebuild. More kids to inspire. But already, what they've achieved is monumental.

They've taken a small-town club and made it a global symbol. Not of wealth or fame—but of heart.

And in doing so, they've reminded us all why we fell in love with this game in the first place.

Battleground of the National League

In the annals of football history, certain stories endure—not merely because of the trophies lifted or records shattered, but because they speak to something deeper. They remind us why we care. Why we cheer. Why we cry. Among those stories, Wrexham AFC's resurgence from the depths of the National League to a place of newfound glory stands tall—a tale not only of football, but of faith, grit, and resurrection.

Founded in 1864, Wrexham isn't just any football club. It is a cornerstone of Welsh sporting heritage—the oldest club in Wales and one of the oldest professional football clubs in the world. Its home, the Racecourse Ground, has witnessed generations of dreams played out on its historic turf. For decades, Wrexham stood proud, competing in the Football League, representing its people with passion and purpose.

But football, like life, can be unforgiving.

In 2008, after years of financial instability, managerial missteps, and heartbreaking near-misses, Wrexham were relegated from the Football League. It wasn't just a drop in status—it was a fall into the unknown. The National League, England's fifth tier, is a punishing landscape. It's a world away from the bright lights of the Premier League. A place where ambition battles scarcity. Where clubs operate on shoestring budgets. Where matches are played in pouring rain in front of modest crowds. Where dreams often go to fade.

For Wrexham, the descent was brutal. Once rubbing shoulders with the likes of West Ham, Stoke, and Newcastle in memorable FA Cup runs, the club now faced long away trips to places like Aldershot and

Welcome to *Wrexham*: The Rise of the Red Dragons

Braintree. The crowds at the Racecourse dwindled. The echoes of past glories hung heavy in the air.

And yet, through it all, one thing never wavered: the fans.

The people of Wrexham, resilient and loyal, stood by their club with unwavering devotion. Through administrative chaos, through relegation battles, through seasons of promise that ended in despair—they were there. Singing. Hoping. Believing. This wasn't just a football club. It was a piece of them.

The National League became a purgatory of sorts. Season after season, Wrexham battled for promotion. In 2011, they came agonizingly close, finishing second—only to lose in the play-offs. That pattern repeated. Moments of hope dashed by cruel endings. Penalty shootouts. Late goals. Managerial changes. Financial struggles. But never surrender.

Then, in 2020, a seismic shift occurred—though not from the pitch.

Hollywood actors Ryan Reynolds and Rob McElhenney, drawn by the club's story and the town's spirit, initiated their now-famous takeover. Many were skeptical. Some were excited. But everyone knew this: things were about to change.

With new ownership came fresh energy. And crucially, a plan.

Rob and Ryan weren't there to paper over cracks. They were there to rebuild from the ground up. Their vision was long-term, but their ambition was immediate. They invested in infrastructure, brought in experienced football minds, and made clear their goal: promotion.

Phil Parkinson, a battle-tested manager with a reputation for building tough, disciplined squads, was brought in to lead the charge. And under his guidance, a new chapter began.

The 2021–22 season was electric. The Racecourse was rocking again. Fans, newly energized by the global attention and renewed hope, filled the stands week after week. Goals flowed. But once again, promotion slipped through Wrexham's grasp. They reached the play-offs, only to fall to Grimsby Town in a 5–4 extra-time thriller—a dagger to the heart in front of their own fans.

Painful. But not fatal.

Instead of despair, there was defiance. The foundation was strong. The belief, even stronger.

Wrexham roared into the 2022–23 season with one goal: get out of the National League. Nothing else would suffice. And this time, the pieces clicked.

The squad was a blend of experience and hunger. Paul Mullin, the talismanic striker signed from Cambridge United, led the line with fire in his boots and ice in his veins. His goals—each one more vital than the last—became symbols of Wrexham's relentless march. Behind him, players like Ollie Palmer, Ben Tozer, and Aaron Hayden brought steel and leadership.

But it wasn't just talent—it was unity. The dressing room believed. The town believed. The world watched.

The league campaign became one of the most thrilling title races in recent memory. Notts County, a fellow sleeping giant, pushed Wrexham to the brink. Both teams shattered records. Both played dazzling football. For months, they traded places at the summit. Every match felt like a final.

And then came *the* game.

April 10, 2023. Wrexham vs. Notts County. Top of the table. Everything on the line.

It was a match of biblical drama. Goals. Lead changes. Moments of pure magic. And in the final minute, with Wrexham leading 3–2, came a penalty for Notts. Silence. Tension. Fear. But then—heroics. Goalkeeper Ben Foster, who had come out of retirement to join the cause, guessed right. Saved it. The Racecourse exploded. History tilted.

That night felt like destiny inching closer.

Just weeks later, it was confirmed. After 15 long, agonizing years in exile, Wrexham were champions of the National League. Promotion secured. The curse lifted.

Tears flowed—not just in Wrexham, but across the globe. Fans who had suffered in silence finally had their moment. The club was back. The town was alive.

Ryan Reynolds wept. Rob McElhenney clutched a pint, overwhelmed. Ben Foster grinned like a kid. Paul Mullin roared. The Racecourse ground, soaked in champagne and joy, felt like the center of the footballing universe.

Wrexham had done more than win a league. They had reclaimed their identity.

The story of their rise from the National League is one of resilience—of never giving up, no matter how long the odds. It's about a town refusing to be forgotten. A club refusing to die. A community rising with its team.

And in a sport often dominated by money, cynicism, and short-term thinking, Wrexham reminded the world what football is *really* about.

Heart.

The Descent into Non-League Football

The echoes of Wrexham AFC's fall from grace reverberated far beyond the stands of the Racecourse Ground. In 2008, the club's relegation from the Football League after 87 years of participation was not just the end of a chapter—it was a harsh, jolting descent into the unknown. It was a moment that would shape the destiny of the club for years to come, testing the very soul of Wrexham AFC and its loyal supporters.

For those who had witnessed Wrexham's glory years, the relegation was more than a sporting setback; it felt like a betrayal of everything the club represented. Once a force to be reckoned with in the Football League, Wrexham now found themselves plunged into the National League, a fifth-tier competition that seemed a world away from the hallowed grounds of English football's top tiers. The race for survival in the National League was grueling and unforgiving. In a league that is often described as a battleground for clubs fighting to stay relevant, Wrexham's pride was put to the test every season.

It was clear from the outset that the road ahead would be anything but easy. The financial instability that had plagued the club for years only worsened in the non-league era. Without the lucrative television deals and sponsorships that come with higher league status, Wrexham struggled to maintain its competitive edge. Budgets were slashed, key players were sold, and wages were delayed. The club had been operating in crisis mode for too long, with ownership changes and off-field turmoil threatening to derail any hope of a resurgence.

During this time, the club's revolving door of managers only added to the sense of instability. With each new appointment came fresh hopes of revival, only to see those dreams dashed by a combination of poor results, limited resources, and the sheer difficulty of competing in a league packed with hungry, ambitious clubs. From the likes of Dean Saunders to Andy Morrell, the managers came and went, each inheriting a team that lacked the necessary depth and momentum to mount a serious challenge for promotion.

It wasn't just the financial constraints or the lack of managerial continuity that made Wrexham's journey through the National

Welcome to *Wrexham*: The Rise of the Red Dragons

League so difficult—it was the weight of expectation. As a club with a rich history, a proud fanbase, and a fierce sense of identity, Wrexham's supporters expected nothing less than a return to the Football League. The club's fall from grace was not only a blow to the team, but also to the community that had long identified with it. For generations, Wrexham AFC had been a symbol of pride, a representation of the town's heart and soul. Yet now, they were languishing in non-league football, battling teams with smaller fanbases and fewer resources.

Despite the hardship, the Wrexham supporters remained a constant force of passion and loyalty. Whether it was a rain-soaked Tuesday night in Grimsby or a chilly Saturday afternoon in Dover, the fans were always there—singing, chanting, and showing up in numbers that exceeded the size of the town itself. The love for the club was unwavering, and it was this devotion that provided the heart and soul of the team during those challenging years.

For many of the players who donned the Wrexham jersey during this period, the pressure of representing a once-proud club weighed heavily. Yet, it was clear that despite the struggles, the team's commitment to the cause never faltered. Players such as Danny Wright, Rob Ogleby, and the talismanic goalkeeper, Chris Maxwell, emerged as key figures who kept the club afloat during the darkest of times. While the performances on the pitch were often inconsistent, the spirit and resilience displayed by the players offered hope in an otherwise bleak period.

However, the impact of non-league football was not solely felt on the field—it resonated deeply within the town. The club's struggles mirrored the challenges faced by the people of Wrexham themselves. A town once proud of its industrial roots and footballing heritage now grappled with economic decline and social change. The rise of globalization had left many small towns like Wrexham feeling disconnected from the modern world, and this disillusionment seeped into the club's fortunes.

Yet, through the pain, there were glimmers of hope. Every now and then, a cup run would rekindle excitement. The FA Cup remained a competition that held a special place in the heart of the Wrexham faithful, and every time the club progressed to a higher round, it felt like a brief escape from the realities of non-league football. These fleeting moments of magic kept the hope alive. And though they came and went, they kept Wrexham's footballing spirit intact.

Perhaps the most defining moment of the club's tenure in the National League came in 2015, when the club reached the play-offs—just one step away from returning to the Football League. The excitement was palpable. The fans believed. The club had the momentum. Yet, as fate often dictates, it was not meant to be. Wrexham fell short, succumbing to a devastating defeat in the play-off final against a resilient Eastleigh side. Once again, promotion slipped through their fingers. This was not just another season lost; it was a crushing blow to the aspirations of the club and its supporters.

Still, the heart of Wrexham AFC continued to beat. Through each setback, through every year of disappointment, the community remained committed to the club. They knew that football had a way of testing the limits of endurance—and in Wrexham, endurance was something that had been built into the very fabric of the town.

The years spent in the National League were tough. The club struggled in ways that went far beyond what anyone could have imagined when Wrexham first fell into the fifth tier. Yet, amid the trials and tribulations, the supporters never gave up. In fact, their belief in the club only grew stronger as time went on.

The descent into non-league football wasn't simply a matter of a club's poor performance—it was a test of character, of loyalty, and of passion. Wrexham AFC may have been relegated from the

Football League, but the essence of the club, its legacy, and the loyalty of its fans were never relegated. They remained as resolute as ever, holding out for the day when Wrexham AFC would rise once more.

Little did they know, this would be the foundation for an epic story of redemption—one that would see Wrexham AFC return to prominence in a way no one could have predicted.

The Hollywood Takeover

In the world of football, ownership changes often go unnoticed or are seen as nothing more than a business transaction. But when Hollywood icons Ryan Reynolds and Rob McElhenney stepped into the fray in 2020, the story of Wrexham AFC took an unexpected and captivating turn that captured the imagination of football fans around the world.

The announcement that Reynolds and McElhenney were set to purchase the historic Welsh club came as a surprise to many, especially given their lack of direct experience in football management. Yet, as the duo emphasized in their initial communications, their involvement was driven by passion rather than profit. Their love for sports, coupled with a deep respect for the community, became the cornerstone of their vision for Wrexham AFC.

Ryan Reynolds, the Canadian actor known for his roles in "Deadpool" and "The Proposal," and Rob McElhenney, the creator and star of "It's Always Sunny in Philadelphia," shared a common belief: to breathe new life into the club, they needed to connect with the fans, restore Wrexham's rich history, and build a sustainable future for the team. Their approach was refreshingly different from the typical corporate takeovers that had become the norm in the world of football. Transparency, community engagement, and respect for the club's traditions were not just buzzwords—they were the foundation upon which they built their new era.

The takeover was completed in February 2021, marking a new chapter in the club's storied history. Fans, initially skeptical, began to warm to the idea of the Hollywood duo at the helm. It was a bold gamble, but for many, it felt like a dream come true—a lifeline thrown to a club that had been struggling for years. Reynolds and McElhenney's promise of "returning Wrexham to its glory days" was not just a statement of intent—it was a declaration of belief in the potential of the club and its community.

Building a Competitive Squad

One of the first and most important steps for Reynolds and McElhenney was to ensure that the club's on-field performances matched the renewed optimism off the field. Under the new ownership, significant investments were made to strengthen Wrexham AFC's squad, bringing in a blend of experienced players and fresh talent to lay the foundation for a competitive team.

One of the standout signings was Paul Mullin, a prolific striker who had been the top scorer in League Two before joining Wrexham. Mullin's arrival sent a clear message that the club was serious about its ambitions. The forward's impressive record at his previous clubs made him a marquee signing, and his addition to the squad was met with excitement from fans eager to see the team compete at a higher level. His goal-scoring ability was the spark that the team needed, and Mullin's presence in the dressing room also provided a wealth of experience that was invaluable to his teammates.

Alongside Mullin, defender Ben Tozer was another key acquisition. Known for his leadership and composure under pressure, Tozer quickly became a rock at the back for Wrexham. His no-nonsense defensive style and ability to organize the team from the back made him an essential part of the squad. The addition of such a strong and commanding figure in defense helped to solidify a unit that had often been inconsistent in previous seasons.

But it wasn't just the big-name signings that were important; it was the philosophy of blending new talent with existing players who had a deep love for the club. Manager Dean Keates, although later replaced by Phil Parkinson, had already begun to work with a squad that showed promise. Under the new ownership, however, that promise began to be fully realized, with the club now having the resources and support to challenge for promotion.

The arrival of Reynolds and McElhenney marked a cultural shift in how Wrexham AFC operated. Where once there was a sense of uncertainty, now there was a clear plan for success. The investments made not only brought quality players to the team but also improved the club's infrastructure, training facilities, and overall support systems. Wrexham was no longer a club teetering on the brink of survival; it was a club with a vision, driven by the belief that they could rise again to the heights they once knew.

A New Era Begins

As the team began to take shape, Reynolds and McElhenney's influence could be seen not just in the boardroom but in the dressing room and on the training field. Their hands-on approach and genuine interest in the well-being of the players were refreshing for the squad. The duo was often spotted at training sessions, talking with players, getting to know them, and offering their support. They were not just owners; they were involved in the day-to-day of the club, showing a level of dedication rarely seen from owners of professional football teams.

The change was also reflected in the club's growing global profile. The combination of Hollywood glamour and a passionate football fanbase proved to be a winning formula. Wrexham AFC's story, from the brink of collapse to a Hollywood-backed revival, began to capture the attention of football fans far and wide. The club's social media presence exploded, with millions of followers tuning in to watch the journey unfold. Reynolds and McElhenney embraced the power of storytelling, using platforms like Twitter, Instagram, and their hit documentary series, *Welcome to Wrexham*, to document every step of the process.

The documentary series, which gave fans an intimate look behind the scenes of Wrexham AFC's ownership and the trials and tribulations of their first season, became a global sensation. Fans from across the globe tuned in to witness the highs and lows of the club's transformation, finding themselves emotionally invested in the journey. The series not only increased the club's visibility but also created an emotional connection between the fans and the club's ownership. The bond between Reynolds, McElhenney, and the Wrexham community grew stronger by the day.

The Road to Redemption

As the 2021-2022 season unfolded, Wrexham AFC's on-field performances began to reflect the investment and energy that had been poured into the club. The team's competitive spirit, combined with the leadership of the new signings and the unwavering support of the fans, pushed the club towards the top of the National League. Wrexham was no longer just a club fighting for survival; they were a club with purpose and the ambition to return to the Football League.

The Hollywood takeover had transformed Wrexham AFC from a struggling lower-league club into a beacon of hope and ambition. The club's resurgence was not just a story of financial investment— it was a story of passion, vision, and the power of community. As Reynolds and McElhenney made clear from the outset, this was about more than just football. It was about revitalizing a town, reconnecting with a community, and creating something that could inspire people around the world.

With every win, every goal, and every new fan added to the club's ever-expanding global family, it became increasingly clear that

Welcome to *Wrexham*: The Rise of the Red Dragons

Wrexham AFC was on the cusp of something special. This was the beginning of a new era, one that would not just see the club rise to new heights but also remind the world of the unbreakable bond between football and community.

For Wrexham, the future was bright. The Hollywood takeover had set the stage for a thrilling new chapter, and with each passing season, it was becoming clearer that the club's best days were ahead of them.

The 2021–2022 Season: Near Miss

The 2021–2022 season marked a turning point for Wrexham AFC. Under the ownership of Ryan Reynolds and Rob McElhenney, the club entered the campaign with a renewed sense of ambition, eager to end their 15-year absence from the Football League. From the outset, the atmosphere around the team was electric. The arrival of new signings, a revitalized fanbase, and a clear vision for the club's future set the stage for an unforgettable season. Yet, as the season unfolded, it became clear that success would not come easy— nothing in football ever does.

Wrexham's journey through the 2021–2022 season was nothing short of thrilling. The squad, bolstered by a mix of experienced players and talented newcomers, demonstrated resilience, grit, and an unyielding belief in their ability to rise through the ranks. Led by manager Phil Parkinson, who had taken the reins in the wake of Dean Keates's departure, Wrexham quickly became one of the most exciting teams in the National League. Parkinson's experience at clubs such as Bradford City, where he had led the team to promotion, proved to be invaluable in guiding Wrexham through the rigors of the non-league season.

From the first whistle of the season, it was clear that Wrexham had the tools to mount a serious challenge for promotion. The team's attacking play was explosive, and their defense, marshaled by the likes of Ben Tozer and Aaron Hayden, was resolute. The club's new signings, including prolific striker Paul Mullin and the dynamic midfielder James Jones, brought an added level of quality and depth to the squad. Mullin's clinical finishing quickly made him a fan favorite, and his partnership with the likes of Ollie Palmer in attack was one of the key highlights of the season.

The Red Dragons started the season with an impressive run of form, regularly dispatching their opponents with ease. Key victories against some of the league's top sides, including Notts County and Chesterfield, showcased Wrexham's growing strength and tactical maturity. Every match was a statement that Wrexham AFC was a club on the rise, and with Reynolds and McElhenney's hands-on involvement, the passion from the boardroom filtered through to the players on the pitch.

Wrexham's home ground, the historic Racecourse Ground, had never looked more alive. The fans, who had long been starved of success, filled the stands with a renewed sense of hope. The atmosphere at home matches became electrifying, with supporters loudly backing their team and reminding the players of the immense pride they carried in wearing the Wrexham shirt. It was a season of belief—a belief that they could reach the promised land of the Football League once more.

However, as the season progressed, it became evident that the National League was an unforgiving battleground, with fierce competition coming from all directions. The top of the table was a tight race, and every point was hard-earned. Wrexham found themselves locked in an intense battle with Stockport County for the coveted automatic promotion spot. In the final weeks of the season, the race for first place went down to the wire.

In the end, despite Wrexham's best efforts, they fell just short of automatic promotion, finishing second behind Stockport County.

Welcome to *Wrexham*: The Rise of the Red Dragons

The disappointment was palpable, as the team had shown enough promise to suggest they deserved to take their place in the Football League. But while finishing second was an achievement in itself, it left a bitter taste—especially considering the automatic promotion spot had been within their grasp.

Wrexham's failure to secure an automatic place meant they would have to navigate the treacherous waters of the playoffs. It was a system that often left no room for error—a single slip could dash the dreams of an entire season. For a club like Wrexham, the pressure was immense, and the sense of anticipation surrounding their playoff campaign was overwhelming.

The playoff semi-finals pitted Wrexham against Grimsby Town—a club with its own storied history and aspirations of returning to the Football League. The first leg of the semi-finals at the Racecourse Ground was a fiercely contested affair, with both teams battling for supremacy. Wrexham put in a strong performance, but it wasn't enough to overcome the resolute Grimsby defense. Despite a valiant effort, Wrexham fell to a 2–1 defeat, leaving them with a mountain to climb in the second leg.

In the return leg at Grimsby's Blundell Park, Wrexham fought valiantly, but the tie slipped from their grasp. A heartbreaking 5–4 aggregate loss sealed their fate, and with it, the club's dreams of automatic promotion were dashed. For the players, staff, and supporters, it was a devastating blow. The pain of coming so close, only to fall short at the final hurdle, was almost unbearable. The emotion in the stands was palpable as the final whistle blew. Fans had given everything—cheering, singing, and believing that this was finally their time. But football, as always, had other plans.

A Heartbreaking Playoff Semi-Final Loss

The heartbreak of the playoff semi-final loss to Grimsby Town highlighted the fine margins that separate success from failure in football. It was a reminder that the road to promotion was filled with obstacles—some within the club's control, others outside of it. For Wrexham, the result was a bitter pill to swallow, but it also underscored the resilience that had been a hallmark of their journey that season.

Despite the loss, the team's performance throughout the year was a source of immense pride. They had proven themselves to be one of the top teams in the National League, and their thrilling style of play had captured the hearts of fans not just in Wrexham but across the football world. There was a sense that, although promotion had eluded them, they were on the right path.

Ryan Reynolds and Rob McElhenney were devastated by the result, but their commitment to the club remained unwavering. In the face of disappointment, they reaffirmed their dedication to the long-term vision of Wrexham AFC. The following season would offer a new opportunity—a chance to build on the lessons learned and continue pushing for that long-awaited return to the Football League.

While the 2021–2022 season ended in heartbreak, it also laid the groundwork for an even brighter future for Wrexham AFC. The club had shown it could compete at the highest level of non-league football. The squad had developed a winning mentality, and the club's infrastructure was in a position to support future success.

As the summer of 2022 approached, the focus shifted to preparing for another push for promotion. With the backing of Reynolds and McElhenney, the club could look ahead with confidence, knowing that the foundations had been laid for a successful campaign. The near miss in the playoffs only fueled the desire to succeed even more.

Wrexham AFC had come so close to returning to the Football League, and with their Hollywood owners leading the charge, the club was poised for another tilt at promotion. The pain of the playoff loss would eventually fade, replaced by the hope that Wrexham's story was far from over. The 2021–2022 season may have been one of near-miss, but it was also a story of triumph, of resilience, and of a club that refused to give up on its dreams.

The 2022–2023 Season: Redemption and Triumph

The 2022–2023 season became a story of redemption for Wrexham AFC. After the heartbreak of coming so close to promotion in the previous year, the club entered the new season with renewed focus, a stronger squad, and a single-minded determination to make up for the near-miss. The pain of the previous season's playoff heartbreak had become the catalyst for this exceptional campaign. Wrexham's players, under the astute management of Phil Parkinson, were not only determined to bounce back but to do so in spectacular fashion.

A Renewed Sense of Purpose

The 2021–2022 season had proven that Wrexham had the quality to compete at the highest level of non-league football. But it also revealed areas where the team needed to improve. The heartbreak of falling short in the playoff semi-finals became the fuel for the club's fire, and with it, an unshakable resolve to secure automatic promotion without relying on the unpredictable lottery of the playoffs.

From the first game of the season, it was clear that Wrexham meant business. Their attacking play was dazzling, and the defense had tightened up, with more resolute performances at the back. The team had learned from the previous year's failures, and the sense of belief that had been so palpable during their impressive 2021–2022 campaign had only grown stronger. The squad exuded confidence, yet there was an understanding that their ultimate goal—promotion to the Football League—would require everything they had.

The Mullin Effect

Welcome to *Wrexham*: The Rise of the Red Dragons

At the heart of Wrexham's attacking prowess was Paul Mullin, whose performances continued to set the standard for the rest of the squad. After an extraordinary season in 2021–2022, where he had already made a massive impact as one of the league's top scorers, Mullin elevated his game to new heights. His eye for goal and unrelenting drive in front of the net made him the focal point of Wrexham's attacking play. With each match, Mullin delivered the kind of performances that would make him a National League legend.

Whether it was his poise in finishing or his tenacity in chasing down defenders, Mullin had become the kind of player who could turn a game on its head in a moment's notice. His partnership with Ollie Palmer, who had himself become a key figure in the attack, was devastating. Together, they formed an attacking duo that struck fear into the hearts of National League defenders. Mullin's ability to score in a variety of ways—whether with his feet or head—meant that Wrexham always had a reliable source of goals.

Throughout the season, Mullin's contributions were more than just goals. He became the talismanic figure of the team, constantly pushing his teammates to reach new levels. The energy he brought to the pitch was contagious. Every time the team needed a spark or a moment of inspiration, Mullin was there, leading by example and setting the tone.

Strengthening the Squad

While Mullin continued to shine, the squad was not just reliant on one player. Under the careful stewardship of Phil Parkinson, Wrexham had built a balanced and cohesive team that could strike in all areas of the pitch. Key acquisitions during the summer bolstered the squad, adding depth and experience.

Ben Tozer, the commanding central defender who had been instrumental in the previous season's performances, remained a constant figure at the back. His leadership and aerial dominance gave Wrexham a rock-solid defense that would prove essential throughout the campaign. Aaron Hayden's partnership with Tozer continued to flourish, with the pair becoming one of the most formidable defensive units in the league.

In midfield, Wrexham boasted a creative engine room that was both disciplined and dynamic. James Jones, alongside the ever-reliable Luke Young, formed a midfield partnership that balanced creative flair with defensive responsibility. The duo orchestrated the play, dictating the tempo and ensuring that the team remained competitive, both in possession and out of it.

The strength in depth was also evident across the pitch. Players such as Jordan Davies, who had been a constant attacking threat, and Tom O'Connor, whose versatility added a tactical edge, ensured that Wrexham's squad was well-equipped for the rigors of the long season. Every member of the team knew their role, and it was this collective approach that allowed Wrexham to stay consistently at the top of the table.

An Explosive Start

The season kicked off with a statement of intent from Wrexham. They stormed through their early fixtures with ease, racking up impressive wins and showing a fluidity in attack that had been honed over the previous year. The team's opening matches were a joy to watch for the fans, who had been yearning for such displays after years of struggle. The attacking style was fast, direct, and clinical, and the defense—while resolute—was occasionally called into action to maintain the balance. It was clear that Wrexham's ambitions were now firmly set on winning the National League title and securing their long-awaited return to the Football League.

With each passing month, the wins kept rolling in. The team's resolve was evident as they fought tooth and nail for every point.

Welcome to *Wrexham*: The Rise of the Red Dragons

Key moments included stunning victories away to some of the league's strongest teams, where Wrexham's attacking brilliance and tactical discipline were on full display. Their relentless pursuit of the top spot saw them build an unassailable lead at the summit of the National League table, gradually pushing other teams out of contention for automatic promotion.

The club's momentum was palpable. As the season progressed, Wrexham's performances became a celebration of everything that had been restored to the club—a sense of pride, purpose, and hope. Their fans, who had been at the heart of every step of the journey, rallied behind the team, creating an atmosphere that was nothing short of electric. Wrexham's rise through the ranks was being driven not only by the quality of their football but also by the emotional connection between the players, the fans, and the club's new owners, Ryan Reynolds and Rob McElhenney.

Record-Breaking Campaign

As the season reached its conclusion, Wrexham's relentless form showed no signs of slowing down. The team's attacking brilliance continued to shine, and the defensive solidity remained unyielding. With each victory, the club moved closer to securing the National League title. The dream of promotion to the Football League was becoming a reality.

On the final day of the season, Wrexham faced their final challenge—securing the one last point needed to clinch the title. The Racecourse Ground was packed with eager fans, every one of them hoping to witness the moment the club's fate would be sealed. In a tense and thrilling encounter, Wrexham triumphed, claiming a 3–1 victory that secured their place at the top of the National League and, more importantly, their promotion to the Football League after a 15-year absence.

Welcome to *Wrexham*: The Rise of the Red Dragons

Wrexham's triumph was more than just a title—it was a redemption story. The club had risen from the ashes of near despair and emerged stronger than ever before. The players, the fans, and the owners had achieved the impossible together. With 111 points, a National League record, Wrexham had not only secured their promotion but had done so in the most emphatic way imaginable.

A Legacy Reborn

The 2022–2023 season will go down in history as one of the most remarkable campaigns in the club's storied history. It was a season where redemption was achieved, a season where a community came together to celebrate a shared dream. For Ryan Reynolds, Rob McElhenney, and the fans of Wrexham AFC, it was a moment of immense pride—a moment where the impossible was made possible.

The title triumph was not just about winning promotion; it was about restoring Wrexham AFC to its rightful place in the Football League. It was a testament to the power of vision, commitment, and community. As the celebrations raged on at the Racecourse Ground, Wrexham AFC's future was brighter than ever.

For the fans, the 2022–2023 season was more than just a record-breaking achievement. It was the realization of a dream, one that had seemed distant for so long but had finally come to fruition. The triumph was not just about football; it was about proving that with passion, perseverance, and a little bit of Hollywood magic, anything was possible.

Community Engagement and Global Recognition

Wrexham AFC's resurgence under the ownership of Ryan Reynolds and Rob McElhenney is a story of transformation that goes beyond the football pitch. It's a tale of revitalizing a football club with a deep connection to its community and using the power of storytelling to bring that journey to the global stage. The ownership duo understood the importance of not only improving the squad but also engaging with the local community, establishing a sense of ownership, and reconnecting the club with its rich history.

The Power of Storytelling: Welcome to Wrexham

The club's meteoric rise under Reynolds and McElhenney reached new heights thanks to the launch of the documentary series *Welcome to Wrexham*, which premiered in 2022. The series offered an inside look at the challenges and triumphs of the new ownership, their vision for the future, and the undying passion of the club's fans. But it was not just a typical sports documentary—it became a global phenomenon that captured the hearts of audiences around the world.

The decision to allow cameras to follow the owners and the team throughout their journey was a bold one, but it paid off in spades. The series showcased not only the behind-the-scenes action at Wrexham AFC but also the human side of the story: the unwavering commitment of the players, the hardships faced by the club, and the everyday people whose lives were touched by the club's success. It highlighted the emotional connection between Wrexham AFC and the people of Wrexham, offering a heartwarming glimpse into the town's community spirit.

A New Global Audience

While Wrexham had always enjoyed a loyal following, the *Welcome to Wrexham* series significantly expanded the club's global reach. Viewers from the United States, Canada, and beyond became invested in the team's story, and the allure of Hollywood-backed owners only fueled the intrigue. Fans from all over the world tuned in to see not just the highs and lows of a football season but the story of two unlikely heroes—Reynolds and McElhenney—stepping into the world of football with no prior experience but with a deep love for the community they had come to embrace.

Welcome to *Wrexham*: The Rise of the Red Dragons

As the series progressed, it became clear that Wrexham's story was not just about football. It was a story about people coming together, about dreams being realized, and about a community that refused to give up. This message resonated with audiences far and wide, sparking a movement of new fans who became dedicated to following the club's progress.

The newfound attention from global viewers also translated into a surge in social media followers, with Wrexham AFC becoming a social media sensation. Celebrities, football fans, and people from all walks of life began following the club's journey, sharing in its triumphs and setbacks. The club's social media accounts became vibrant spaces for international fans to engage with the team and with each other, solidifying Wrexham's status as a global football brand.

Wrexham as a Symbol of Resilience

While the documentary series brought international fame, the essence of Wrexham's story remained rooted in resilience, perseverance, and community. The club's rise from the National League to the Football League was a triumph for everyone involved—the owners, the players, the fans, and the people of Wrexham. It was a reminder that, with the right vision and collective effort, anything is possible, no matter how daunting the challenge may seem.

The community of Wrexham has always been the beating heart of the club, and under Reynolds and McElhenney's stewardship, that bond only grew stronger. The new owners made a conscious effort to engage with the local community, visiting schools, meeting with supporters, and actively participating in the life of the town. Their commitment to transparency and to listening to the fans allowed them to forge a strong relationship with the people of Wrexham, who were integral to the club's revival.

Welcome to *Wrexham*: The Rise of the Red Dragons

In addition to supporting the team on matchdays, the Wrexham community took an active role in the club's success. From local businesses to schools, Wrexham AFC became a source of pride and unity. The club became a symbol of what could be achieved when a community came together with purpose and belief. The narrative of a small town fighting for its place in the football world resonated deeply, reminding people around the world that football is more than just a game—it's a powerful force that can bring people together and change lives.

A Global Movement: Wrexham's International Fanbase

As Wrexham's profile continued to rise, the club's fanbase began to expand in ways that no one could have predicted. The documentary series played a crucial role in attracting fans from across the globe, many of whom had never previously heard of Wrexham AFC. As interest grew, so did the international presence of the club. Fans from the United States, Australia, and other parts of Europe began purchasing Wrexham AFC merchandise, wearing the club's colors with pride, and supporting the team from afar.

Wrexham's journey transcended borders, as fans from all over the world found common ground in their support for the club. Social media platforms became an outlet for fans to share their excitement, celebrate victories, and discuss the club's prospects. The fanbase became a diverse, global family, united by their love for Wrexham AFC and their shared dream of seeing the club return to the Football League.

The influence of Wrexham's international fanbase was undeniable. With thousands of new supporters rallying behind the team, the club's profile grew not just on a local level but on a global scale. It wasn't just about football anymore; Wrexham had become a symbol of hope, of community, and of the power of sports to unite people across cultures.

Welcome to *Wrexham*: The Rise of the Red Dragons

A Legacy of Transformation

The rise of Wrexham AFC serves as a testament to the transformative power of community and perseverance. What began as an ambitious vision by Reynolds and McElhenney—to restore a historic football club to its former glory—has blossomed into something much bigger. The story of Wrexham AFC is not just about two Hollywood stars coming to the rescue of a football club— it is about the collective strength of a community that refuses to be forgotten, the vision of owners who cared more about people than profits, and the global recognition that came as a result of their efforts.

The club's journey exemplifies the incredible potential of football to unite people, inspire dreams, and create lasting change. In many ways, Wrexham's story has become a blueprint for how clubs, communities, and individuals can achieve greatness, no matter the obstacles in their path.

As Wrexham continues to rise, their story will remain an inspiration for those who believe in the power of vision, passion, and community—reminding us all that sometimes, the most improbable of dreams can come true.

The Fears and Misconceptions of the National League

Welcome to *Wrexham*: The Rise of the Red Dragons

To the uninitiated, the National League is just "non-league football"—a term that evokes images of muddy pitches, half-empty stands, and Sunday-league-level quality. But to those who've experienced it—players, managers, fans, and club owners—it is a crucible of character, an unforgiving battleground, and a test of dreams versus reality. It's also one of the most misunderstood levels of the English football pyramid.

In this chapter, we explore the fears and misconceptions associated with the National League—often dubbed "football's Bermuda Triangle," where big clubs can vanish from relevance, and promotion can feel like climbing Everest without oxygen.

Misconception 1: "It's Amateur Football"

One of the biggest misconceptions about the National League is that it's amateur or semi-professional. In truth, many National League clubs are fully professional. Clubs like Wrexham, Notts County, and Chesterfield have professional infrastructures, full-time players, and thousands of fans packing into their stadiums.

Yet the stigma remains. The word "non-league" conjures condescending notions. This false perception becomes a psychological barrier for players who drop down from League Two or above. It's seen as a fall from grace. But the truth is far more complex. Players here train just as hard, feel just as much pressure, and play in atmospheres every bit as electric—especially when something is at stake.

This misconception also filters into media coverage, which often neglects National League fixtures unless a former Premier League name is involved. The reality is: the league is professional, passionate, and fiercely competitive.

Misconception 2: "Getting Promoted Is Easy"

Many owners and fans—especially those new to football or unfamiliar with the league—assume that a well-funded club with decent players will breeze through the division. But the National League is notoriously hard to escape. Only two teams go up: one automatically and one through the play-offs, which are brutal and unpredictable.

It doesn't matter how big your club is or how many fans you have. Just ask clubs like Stockport County, Grimsby Town, or Wrexham—all with rich histories—how long they lingered in the league. Being the biggest fish in the pond doesn't guarantee success.

This tight bottleneck means even an impressive season can end in heartbreak. A club could finish second with 90+ points and still miss promotion because of one bad day in the playoffs.

Misconception 3: "Money Buys Promotion"

While investment certainly helps—better facilities, stronger squads, professional support staff—it doesn't guarantee anything. The National League is not just about skill or spending. It's about adaptability, mentality, and grinding out results on windy Tuesdays in February.

Clubs with significant financial backing have struggled here. The league is full of seasoned managers, well-drilled teams, and players hungry to prove themselves. These are men playing for their livelihood. It's not a division where you can outspend your way to success easily.

In fact, overspending has led many clubs to financial ruin. Some gamble everything on a promotion push, fail, and collapse. The pressure to escape often leads to rash decisions, and the league punishes impatience.

Fear 1: "Once You're Down Here, You're Forgotten"

Perhaps the biggest fear among relegated clubs is irrelevance. Dropping out of the Football League can feel like falling off a cliff. There's a real worry that sponsors, media coverage, and supporters will disappear.

And sometimes, they do.

Many fans distance themselves out of disappointment. Sponsors pull out. The media pays less attention. Players leave. Managers resign. It's easy to spiral.

But there are exceptions. Wrexham is a case in point—reinvigorated by passionate ownership and a loyal fanbase. Relevance can be regained, but it takes effort, storytelling, and often, a bit of stardust.

The fear of being forgotten isn't irrational. It's rooted in the league's historical obscurity. But as social media and documentaries have shown, any club—no matter where they play—can be spotlighted if the story is compelling enough.

Fear 2: "We'll Be Stuck Here Forever"

The "non-league graveyard" is a phrase no club wants to hear. It implies stagnation and lost hope. And it's a genuine fear, especially for clubs that have narrowly missed out on promotion year after year. The longer you stay in the National League, the harder it can be to escape.

Momentum is a fragile thing in football. The optimism of relegation ("we'll bounce straight back") often turns into years of frustration. Clubs settle into the league and lose that desperate edge. Budgets are trimmed. Expectations reset. Fans grow cynical.

This fear is amplified by how few clubs get promoted each year. In League Two, four clubs go up. In the Championship, three. But in the National League? Just two. For a league with 24 fiercely competitive sides, it's a brutal math problem.

Misconception 4: "The Football Quality Is Poor"

There is a prevailing belief that National League football is all long balls and rough challenges. While it's certainly more physical than the Premier League, the quality is underrated.

Many players in the league are former EFL professionals. Some are rising talents looking to break through. Teams like Notts County, Barnet, and Eastleigh have been praised for their passing, movement, and tactical discipline. You'll find goal-of-the-season contenders, tight defensive masterclasses, and end-to-end thrillers almost every weekend.

Moreover, modern coaching has filtered down. There are analytics departments, nutritionists, GPS tracking, and performance analysis—even in the fifth tier. The league is evolving, and the football has too.

Fear 3: "One Injury or One Bad Run Can Derail Everything"

Due to smaller squads and tighter budgets, one or two injuries can change a club's season. A key striker goes down in January? It could cost promotion. A goalkeeper has a dip in form? Points are lost. The margin for error is razor-thin.

This instability leads to immense pressure on players and coaching staff. The fear isn't just of failure—it's of misfortune. Unlike the Premier League, where clubs have depth for every position, National League sides often rely heavily on a few key players.

There's also the fear that a brief dip in form will cost someone their job. Managers are sacked quickly. Owners panic. Fans demand change. And in a league where momentum is everything, a five-game winless streak can kill a season.

Fear 4: "Will Anyone Care If We Succeed?"

For many players, especially those nearing the end of their careers or those who've dropped down from higher levels, there's an existential question: **What's the point if no one notices?**

It's a harsh reality. Scoring 20 goals in the National League won't get the same attention as scoring 5 in League Two. Media coverage is limited. National team scouts rarely attend. Even agents can lose interest.

Yet this fear, while understandable, misses the magic of the league. Fans care. Communities care. The promotion celebrations at clubs like Grimsby and Wrexham have shown that success in the National League can be life-changing—for the club, the town, and the players.

Overcoming the Stigma

Breaking free from the fears and misconceptions starts with education and visibility. Documentaries like *Welcome to Wrexham* have helped. They've humanized the players, shown the grind behind the glamour, and proved that compelling football stories exist outside the top tiers.

Club ownership is evolving too. New owners bring modern branding, fan engagement strategies, and a sense of mission. They're rebranding "non-league" not as a failure, but as a beginning. A place to rebuild. A place to rise.

Supporters play a role as well. Fans who stay loyal during these tough years often become the backbone of a club's revival. Their belief counters the fear. Their voices drown out the stigma.

Conclusion: The League of Real Football

The National League is a pressure cooker, a place where dreams teeter on the edge of despair. It's often misjudged, routinely underestimated, and deeply feared by clubs tumbling into it.

But beneath the weight of its fears and misconceptions lies something rare: authenticity.

This is football stripped of glamour, driven by desire. It's Tuesday night battles in the rain, last-minute winners in front of 4,000 fans, and entire towns rising and falling with their team's fate.

For some, it's a prison. For others, a proving ground.

But for all who've passed through it—it's unforgettable.

League Two – A Statement of Intent

Following their remarkable promotion from the National League, Wrexham AFC entered the 2023–24 League Two season with an unwavering sense of purpose and ambition. The club's journey from non-league football to the Football League had already captured the hearts of many, but the real challenge was yet to come. The goal was clear: not just to survive in League Two, but to make an immediate impact and push for back-to-back promotions—a feat that would serve as a testament to the rapid transformation that Wrexham had undergone under the ownership of Hollywood duo Ryan Reynolds and Rob McElhenney.

Season Overview

Wrexham's entrance into League Two was nothing short of a statement. With the weight of expectation on their shoulders, the team did not falter. They finished the season in second place, securing automatic promotion to League One and proving that their rise was no fluke. The squad amassed a total of 88 points, a feat that demonstrated their consistency, resilience, and ability to perform under pressure.

The turning point came on 13 April 2024, when Wrexham sealed their promotion with a resounding 6–0 victory over Forest Green Rovers. This victory, coupled with favorable results from rival teams, confirmed that Wrexham had achieved their goal—securing a second successive promotion. The scoreline itself was a statement of intent, showing that the club had not only arrived in League Two but was capable of challenging the best.

Key Players and Standout Performances

Several standout players were integral to Wrexham's success during the 2023–24 season. The team's top scorer, Paul Mullin, continued his exceptional form from the previous season, contributing crucial goals that helped propel the club up the table. His ability to find the back of the net in key moments made him a focal point of Wrexham's attack, while his work rate and leadership on the field were vital for the team's success.

In defense, Ben Tozer proved to be a rock, offering stability and leadership in the backline. His commanding presence and ability to organize the defense were critical in ensuring that Wrexham remained solid defensively throughout the campaign. Alongside Tozer, the defensive unit, including goalkeeper Rob Lainton, stood firm, keeping crucial clean sheets when it mattered most.

Welcome to *Wrexham*: The Rise of the Red Dragons

In midfield, the creativity and dynamism of Elliot Lee and Jordan Davies were essential to Wrexham's attacking play. Lee's vision and passing range allowed the team to control the tempo of the game, while Davies' energy and flair were often the driving force behind counter-attacks and goal-scoring opportunities.

Tactical Approach and Style of Play

Under manager Phil Parkinson, Wrexham adopted a tactical approach that balanced defensive solidity with attacking ambition. Parkinson's focus on structured defending, coupled with a quick and direct attacking style, helped the team thrive in the highly competitive environment of League Two. The team's ability to play both possession-based football and counter-attacking football allowed them to dominate opponents in a variety of ways.

The emphasis on pressing high up the pitch, particularly in away games, was another key element of their success. Wrexham's forwards and midfielders worked tirelessly to win back possession quickly, forcing opposition teams into mistakes and capitalizing on those opportunities. This relentless work ethic, coupled with clinical finishing, made Wrexham a difficult team to play against.

The Importance of Depth and Squad Rotation

While the first XI performed admirably throughout the season, Wrexham's success was also built on the depth of their squad. Injuries and suspensions are inevitable in any football campaign, but Wrexham's ability to rotate players without a significant drop in quality was key to their promotion push. Players such as Luke Young, Ollie Palmer, and James Jones all made vital contributions from the bench, ensuring that the team maintained its intensity throughout the season.

The strength in depth also allowed Wrexham to compete in a grueling league schedule, where the demand for consistent performances is high. This squad rotation was especially important in the final stages of the season, when the pressure of securing promotion intensified.

The Impact of the Hollywood Owners

Ryan Reynolds and Rob McElhenney's involvement with Wrexham AFC continued to have a profound impact on the club during the 2023–24 season. Their presence brought a unique blend of celebrity and footballing ambition that raised the profile of the club both in the UK and internationally. However, it wasn't just about the glamour and the media attention—Reynolds and McElhenney were deeply invested in the club's success. They attended matches, interacted with fans, and, more importantly, backed the team with strategic financial investments.

Their ownership not only provided the necessary resources to attract top talent but also inspired the players and coaching staff to aim higher. The media attention surrounding their ownership brought additional commercial opportunities, further boosting the club's resources. This financial backing enabled Wrexham to compete on equal terms with other clubs in the division, allowing them to secure the signings that would prove pivotal in their promotion push.

The Significance of the Promotion

Wrexham's automatic promotion to League One was a monumental achievement. It not only marked the continuation of the club's remarkable rise but also served as a validation of the ownership's vision and investment. The significance of this achievement was felt throughout the community, with fans celebrating in the streets of Wrexham after the final whistle against Forest Green Rovers. It was a moment of collective joy, as the hard work of players, staff, and supporters culminated in the ultimate reward—back-to-back promotions.

For the people of Wrexham, this promotion represented more than just a place in the third tier of English football—it was the restoration of pride. It was proof that, with determination and the right leadership, the club could overcome the financial constraints and limitations of non-league football. It was a victory for the town, the fans, and everyone who had supported the club through its darkest times.

Looking Ahead: The Challenge of League One

As Wrexham AFC celebrated their promotion to League One, they were fully aware of the challenges that lay ahead. The competition in the third tier of English football would be fierce, with bigger clubs, higher expectations, and more intense pressure. But for Wrexham, this was just another chapter in a story of resilience, ambition, and transformation.

The club's ownership duo, Reynolds and McElhenney, have already expressed their ambition to push for further success. With the infrastructure in place, the squad ready, and the community behind them, Wrexham's ascent through the English football pyramid seems set to continue. The goal now is not just to survive in League One but to establish themselves as a competitive force and continue their remarkable rise through the leagues.

The 2023–24 season was a defining moment in the history of Wrexham AFC. The club's promotion to League One, achieved with a mixture of skill, determination, and tactical intelligence, demonstrated that the team was ready for the next challenge. Under the stewardship of Ryan Reynolds and Rob McElhenney, Wrexham had not only returned to the Football League but had established themselves as a force to be reckoned with. The journey is far from over, and the next chapter promises to be just as exciting, as Wrexham AFC continues its pursuit of greatness.

Welcome to *Wrexham*: The Rise of the Red Dragons

Key Players and Performances

Wrexham's success during the 2023–24 season was built on a collective effort, but certain individuals stood out, delivering performances that made all the difference in the club's promotion to League One.

Paul Mullin – The Star Striker

Striker Paul Mullin was undoubtedly the standout player of the season. The talismanic forward continued to prove his worth as one of the most prolific goal scorers in English football, finishing as both the League Two top scorer with 24 goals and the season's overall top scorer with 27 goals. His contributions were crucial to Wrexham's attacking success, as he consistently found the back of the net in key moments throughout the campaign.

Mullin's ability to score in a variety of ways, whether through poacher's finishes, long-range strikes, or headers, demonstrated his versatility and footballing intelligence. His leadership and presence on the pitch were equally important, often rallying his teammates and driving them forward in moments of pressure. The Wrexham fans, who had adopted him as one of their own, continued to sing his name as a symbol of the club's renaissance.

Mullin's most memorable performance came in the 6–0 demolition of Morecambe on 25 November 2023, where he scored a brace. His composure and clinical finishing were on full display in that match, which also epitomized Wrexham's attacking potency during the season.

Ben Tozer – The Defensive Leader

While Mullin's goals were essential to Wrexham's promotion push, it was Ben Tozer's leadership and defensive solidity that helped anchor the team throughout the season. As captain, Tozer led by example, both on and off the field, ensuring that the backline remained organized and resilient.

Welcome to *Wrexham*: The Rise of the Red Dragons

Tozer's no-nonsense defending and aerial dominance made him a formidable presence in the heart of the defense. His partnership with fellow defenders such as Aaron Hayden and Max Cleworth was instrumental in Wrexham's impressive defensive record. Throughout the season, the club posted several clean sheets, showcasing their ability to repel attacks and maintain composure in high-pressure situations.

In the decisive 6–0 victory over Forest Green Rovers, Tozer's leadership and organizational skills were on full display. His calmness under pressure helped marshal the team to an emphatic win, securing Wrexham's promotion to League One.

Elliot Lee – The Creative Spark

In the midfield, Elliot Lee continued to be the creative engine driving Wrexham's attacking play. Lee's vision, passing range, and technical ability were key components of the team's ability to break down opposition defenses. His composure on the ball allowed Wrexham to transition quickly from defense to attack, with many of the team's most incisive moves originating from his passes.

Lee also contributed with crucial goals and assists, showcasing his knack for arriving in dangerous positions at the right moments. His link-up play with Mullin and fellow attacking players was a key feature of Wrexham's attacking approach, and his chemistry with the forwards proved to be a constant threat to opponents.

Ollie Palmer – The Target Man

Ollie Palmer's role in the team was often that of a target man, holding up the ball and bringing others into play. His physical presence and aerial ability allowed him to provide a different dynamic to the attack, complementing the more mobile and clinical Mullin. Palmer's strength and heading ability were crucial in situations where Wrexham needed a focal point in attack.

Palmer's contributions extended beyond just goals. His work rate and willingness to battle in the air helped stretch defenses, creating space for his teammates to exploit. In the 6–0 victory over Forest Green Rovers, Palmer's presence in the box contributed to Wrexham's overwhelming dominance.

Rob Lainton – The Dependable Goalkeeper

Wrexham's goalkeeper, Rob Lainton, was another key player whose consistency provided the foundation for the team's success. Lainton's shot-stopping ability and leadership from the back were essential in ensuring that Wrexham remained solid defensively throughout the season.

Lainton's calmness under pressure and ability to organize the defense were pivotal, especially in the tightest of matches. His command of the penalty area allowed his defenders to focus on their tasks without the worry of crosses or set pieces causing unnecessary problems. Lainton's performances in goal were key to Wrexham's promotion, with several crucial saves in big moments helping to preserve vital points.

Standout Performances – Big Victories

Wrexham's attacking prowess was on full display during some of their biggest victories of the season. The 6–0 win against Morecambe on 25 November 2023 was one of the most dominant performances of the campaign. The team's clinical finishing and ability to control the match from start to finish left an indelible mark on both fans and critics alike.

The victory was highlighted by two goals from Paul Mullin, as well as contributions from other players, showcasing the team's attacking depth. The match served as a reminder of the club's growing confidence and ambition in League Two, sending a clear message to the rest of the league that Wrexham was a force to be reckoned with.

Welcome to *Wrexham*: The Rise of the Red Dragons

Equally significant was the 6–0 triumph over Forest Green Rovers on 13 April 2024, which sealed Wrexham's promotion to League One. The comprehensive victory demonstrated not only Wrexham's attacking potency but also their defensive stability. The clean sheet, combined with a relentless attacking display, encapsulated everything that had made Wrexham such a formidable side during the season.

The key players of the 2023–24 season—Paul Mullin, Ben Tozer, Elliot Lee, Ollie Palmer, and Rob Lainton—were instrumental in Wrexham AFC's historic promotion to League One. Their performances, along with the collective effort of the squad, underscored the progress the club had made under the ownership of Ryan Reynolds and Rob McElhenney. With a combination of attacking flair, defensive solidity, and a deep squad, Wrexham AFC proved that they were ready for the challenges of the third tier of English football.

The team's key victories and standout performances highlighted their growing strength and determination, setting the stage for the next chapter in the club's incredible journey.

Attendance and Fan Engagement

One of the most notable aspects of Wrexham AFC's 2023–24 season was the extraordinary support the club received from its passionate fanbase. The team's rise through the ranks, coupled with the widespread attention generated by Hollywood owners Ryan Reynolds and Rob McElhenney, led to a surge in attendance and fan engagement throughout the season.

Highest Attendance: 12,562 vs Stockport County (27 April 2024)

The highest attendance of the season came in a crucial match against Stockport County on 27 April 2024, where 12,562 fans packed the

Welcome to *Wrexham*: The Rise of the Red Dragons

Racecourse Ground. The fixture was not only significant for its role in securing promotion to League One but also symbolized the growing momentum of Wrexham AFC as they aimed for a second consecutive promotion.

This match marked a celebratory atmosphere as fans gathered to witness history in the making. The electric environment in the stands, with supporters singing and chanting in unison, created an unforgettable atmosphere, underscoring the special connection between the club and its community. The match was a testament to Wrexham's resurgence and the unity between the fans, players, and owners.

Lowest Attendance: 4,963 vs Burton Albion (5 December 2023)

Despite the overwhelming support Wrexham enjoyed throughout the season, the club's lowest attendance came in a fixture against Burton Albion on 5 December 2023. With 4,963 fans in attendance, the turnout reflected the natural ebb and flow of attendance throughout the campaign, particularly during mid-week matches or fixtures that fell on less favorable dates for supporters.

Nevertheless, even during such matches, the support remained loyal. The low attendance in no way diminished the sense of community or the passion of those who were present. It was a testament to the club's ability to draw dedicated fans who remained loyal to the team, irrespective of the size of the crowd.

Fan Engagement and the Role of the Documentary

The involvement of Ryan Reynolds and Rob McElhenney has undoubtedly played a significant role in Wrexham's global fan engagement. The documentary series *"Welcome to Wrexham,"* which followed the journey of the club under the Hollywood duo's ownership, brought Wrexham's story to millions of viewers around the world. The series allowed fans, both old and new, to connect

Welcome to *Wrexham*: The Rise of the Red Dragons

with the club on a personal level, offering a behind-the-scenes look at the players, coaches, and, most importantly, the community.

The fans' passion was further ignited by the personalities and charisma of the club's owners, who often engaged directly with supporters through social media and public appearances. Their active involvement in the club's day-to-day operations and transparent communication created a sense of inclusivity, making fans feel like they were part of the journey, not just passive observers.

In addition to the global attention generated by the documentary, Wrexham also capitalized on their growing popularity by expanding their merchandising and creating fan events, which allowed supporters to engage with the club in new and meaningful ways. Special matchday experiences, fan meetups, and fan-driven initiatives became central to the club's efforts to build lasting relationships with its supporters.

The Power of Wrexham's Loyal Fanbase

The loyalty of Wrexham's fanbase cannot be overstated. Throughout the season, whether in record-breaking crowds or smaller, more intimate gatherings, the supporters demonstrated a deep and unwavering commitment to their club. Their passion was evident not only in their vocal support but also in their investment in the future of the team.

The continued attendance and fan engagement reflect the growth of Wrexham AFC from a local football club to a global phenomenon, driven by a strong community spirit. The relationship between Wrexham and its supporters is one built on shared history, collective pride, and a unified vision for the future.

Conclusion

Wrexham's 2023–24 season was not just a triumph on the pitch but also a testament to the club's profound connection with its fanbase. With the highest attendance recorded at 12,562 and the continued strong fan engagement seen throughout the season, it was clear that Wrexham AFC had become more than just a football club—it had become a symbol of community, resilience, and hope.

As the club prepares for its next challenge in League One, the strength of its fanbase will undoubtedly continue to play a pivotal role in Wrexham's pursuit of greater success. Whether in packed stands or more intimate settings, Wrexham's fans will remain a driving force in the club's ongoing journey.

Cup Competitions: A Stepping Stone to Greater Glory

While Wrexham's primary focus in the 2023–24 season was to secure their place in League One, their performance in domestic cup competitions provided both a platform for growth and an opportunity to test their mettle against higher-tier teams. Each cup run served as an important chapter in the club's rise, offering valuable experience for players and management alike.

FA Cup: A Glorious Fourth Round Journey

One of the standout moments of Wrexham's 2023–24 campaign was their impressive run in the FA Cup. The oldest domestic cup competition in the world is always a stage where lower-league clubs like Wrexham can shine and create memorable moments. Wrexham's path through the tournament was nothing short of inspiring.

The team reached the Fourth Round, a notable achievement given the fierce competition from top-flight sides. In the early stages, Wrexham showcased their trademark resilience, overcoming teams from lower divisions with ease and advancing with flair. The Fourth Round was particularly significant as it saw them face off against a top-tier team, showcasing their ability to compete at a higher level. Although they were ultimately knocked out, the team's performance demonstrated their potential to challenge in bigger competitions, and the match captured the hearts of fans.

For the club's supporters, the FA Cup journey brought a renewed sense of belief that their team could mix it with the best. The chance to see Wrexham face off against the likes of Premier League and Championship clubs was a testament to their growth under Ryan Reynolds and Rob McElhenney's ownership. The cup run was an affirmation of the club's ambition to restore its glory and demonstrate its competitiveness beyond the confines of League Two.

EFL Cup: Building Experience in the Domestic Cups

In the EFL Cup (Carabao Cup), Wrexham advanced to the Second Round, where they faced a challenging fixture against a team from the higher divisions. While the team did not progress further, the experience proved invaluable for the squad, especially the younger players and newcomers looking to make their mark.

The EFL Cup offered Wrexham a chance to test their depth and adaptability. The squad rotation and tactical changes provided insight into the team's versatility, allowing manager Phil Parkinson to experiment with formations and tactical approaches against diverse opposition. For the players, it was an opportunity to experience the pace and intensity of cup football, which will serve them well as they embark on future challenges in higher leagues.

The team's progress in the EFL Cup also underscored Wrexham's growing presence in domestic competitions. The cup run, while short, highlighted the club's potential to be a formidable opponent, even when facing teams from leagues above them.

EFL Trophy: Round of 32 – Further Demonstrating Squad Depth

In the EFL Trophy, Wrexham progressed to the Round of 32, further showcasing the depth and versatility of their squad. The EFL Trophy, which features teams from both the Football League and lower divisions, provided Wrexham with another chance to test their strength against a variety of opposition.

Although the competition was not as high-profile as the FA Cup or EFL Cup, it still offered meaningful opportunities for the players to gain match experience. The progression to the Round of 32 was particularly notable because it illustrated the squad's resilience, with Wrexham managing to field competitive line-ups even when rotating players.

The EFL Trophy also allowed Wrexham to give valuable game time to those on the fringes of the first team. For a club with the ambition of Wrexham, depth is essential, and the trophy matches served as a proving ground for young players and those aiming to secure a place in the starting XI.

Cup Competitions: A Foundation for League One Aspirations

While cup glory was not secured in the 2023–24 season, the experience gained in the FA Cup, EFL Cup, and EFL Trophy will stand Wrexham in good stead for the challenges ahead. Each tournament was a vital stepping stone in the club's progression, offering crucial exposure and opportunities for the team to demonstrate their growth.

For Wrexham, these cup runs were more than just a way to bring in prize money or recognition; they were about fostering a competitive mindset that could help the team flourish in the higher tiers of English football. As the club moves into League One for the 2024–25 season, the lessons learned from their cup performances— whether through tough losses or hard-fought victories—will provide invaluable experience.

Conclusion: Strengthening Foundations and Building for the Future

Wrexham's success in cup competitions during the 2023–24 season, combined with their promotion to League One, illustrates the club's upward trajectory and strategic approach to both league and cup football. As they continue to climb the football pyramid, Wrexham's deepening squad depth, invaluable cup experience, and ever-growing fanbase lay a solid foundation for future success.

With their eyes now set on further advancement, including making an impact in League One and beyond, Wrexham AFC's journey is far from over. As they continue to build momentum both on and off the pitch, the experience gained in cup competitions will play a key role in achieving their long-term aspirations. For the fans and the footballing world at large, Wrexham's rise is a story that remains captivating and full of promise.

Welcome to League One

The 2024–25 season marked a historic and momentous chapter for Wrexham AFC: their return to League One after a 20-year absence. Under the astute guidance of manager Phil Parkinson and the transformative ownership of Hollywood duo Ryan Reynolds and Rob McElhenney, the club was determined to build upon their recent successes and continue their incredible rise through the English football pyramid. With the momentum of three consecutive promotions, Wrexham were ready to challenge themselves at a higher level, and their performance in League One more than proved they were up to the task.

Welcome to *Wrexham*: The Rise of the Red Dragons

Season Overview: A Historic Third Consecutive Promotion

The 2024–25 League One campaign will go down in history for Wrexham, not just for their return to the third tier of English football, but for their ability to secure another automatic promotion, this time to the EFL Championship. The team amassed an impressive 89 points, with a remarkable record of 26 wins, 11 draws, and only 8 losses. This achievement marked an unprecedented third consecutive promotion for the club—an extraordinary feat in English football, showcasing the incredible progress made under Reynolds and McElhenney's ownership.

The transition to League One was never going to be easy. The step up from the National League to League Two was challenging enough, but the leap to the third tier of English football required significant adaptability. Nevertheless, Wrexham adapted swiftly, demonstrating their resilience, tactical flexibility, and an ever-growing team cohesion. The squad, which had been carefully strengthened over the previous seasons, was ready to compete with some of the most established teams in the league.

With each victory, Wrexham's confidence soared, and their brand of football became increasingly effective. The attacking play was potent, while the defense proved to be resolute and dependable. Phil Parkinson's tactical nous, combined with the individual brilliance of key players, ensured that Wrexham were not only surviving in League One, but thriving.

Key Matches: Defining Moments of the Season

Several matches during the 2024–25 campaign became defining moments in Wrexham's push for promotion. Each of these key fixtures demonstrated the strength, determination, and potential of the team as they faced off against some of the toughest competition in League One.

26 April 2025: Wrexham 3–0 Charlton Athletic

The 3–0 victory over Charlton Athletic at the STōK Cae Ras on 26 April 2025 was a defining moment of the season, as it confirmed Wrexham's promotion to the EFL Championship. The match was a celebration of all that had been achieved over the past few years, with the atmosphere at the stadium electric and filled with palpable excitement. The dominant performance against Charlton not only sealed the promotion but also served as a statement of intent: Wrexham AFC were not just content with surviving in League One—they were ready to conquer the next challenge.

The game itself was a display of Wrexham's attacking prowess. Paul Mullin continued his remarkable form, scoring one of the goals of the season, and providing an assist in the process. The midfield trio controlled the game with calm authority, and the defense was resolute in keeping a clean sheet against a strong Charlton side. The final whistle was met with wild celebrations from the players, staff, and the passionate Wrexham supporters, who had witnessed the club's remarkable rise from the depths of the National League to the cusp of Championship football.

24 August 2024: Wrexham 3–0 Reading

In only the second month of the season, Wrexham sent a powerful message to the rest of the league with a 3–0 victory over Reading. The match was an early test of the team's credentials, and Wrexham passed with flying colors. The result was particularly impressive because it came against a team with considerable pedigree in the Championship and a solid reputation in League One.

The victory was characterized by a superb team performance, with Wrexham showing their attacking flair and clinical finishing. Paul Mullin was once again on target, scoring a brace that had the fans in raptures. The midfield's creativity shone through, with Jack Payne pulling the strings and setting up key passes. Defensively, Wrexham remained solid, keeping Reading at bay with an organized backline and a standout performance from goalkeeper Ben Foster.

The result established Wrexham as serious contenders for promotion and cemented their place among the league's top teams. The fans were now fully invested in the idea that their club was not just participating in League One but could thrive in it.

5 October 2024: Wrexham 4–1 Northampton Town

A 4–1 victory over Northampton Town on 5 October 2024 was another statement win that highlighted Wrexham's attacking depth and versatility. The match was an absolute masterclass in attacking football, with the team showcasing their ability to break down opposition defenses and convert chances with ruthless efficiency.

Paul Mullin once again found the back of the net, but it was the performances of other players such as Elliot Lee and Luke Young that really caught the eye. Lee was instrumental in pulling the strings from midfield, and his creative vision led to several dangerous attacking moves, while Young's tireless work rate in the center of the park provided the balance needed for Wrexham to dominate possession. The team's performance was rounded off with a superb goal from defender Ben Tozer, who capped off a set-piece move with a header that had the fans singing his praises.

Player Highlights: Key Figures in Wrexham's Historic Campaign

Wrexham's success in the 2024–25 League One season was driven by several key players, each of whom played a crucial role in the team's promotion charge.

Welcome to *Wrexham*: The Rise of the Red Dragons

Paul Mullin – The Prolific Striker

Once again, Paul Mullin was the club's talisman. His incredible goal-scoring form continued, and his ability to find the back of the net when it mattered most was a key factor in Wrexham's promotion. Mullin finished the season as the top scorer, contributing an impressive tally of 28 goals in all competitions. His movement, composure in front of goal, and work ethic made him one of the most lethal strikers in the division.

Ben Tozer – The Defensive Leader

Ben Tozer's leadership at the back was indispensable. His organizational skills and ability to marshal the defense provided a solid foundation for Wrexham's rise. Tozer also chipped in with a few important goals, including his memorable header in the victory over Northampton Town. His presence and composure under pressure made him an invaluable asset to the team.

Elliot Lee – The Creative Playmaker

Elliot Lee's creativity in the midfield was key to unlocking opposition defenses. His vision, passing range, and flair were instrumental in Wrexham's attacking play. Lee formed an excellent partnership with Luke Young, and together they provided the perfect balance between creativity and tenacity in the middle of the park.

Looking Ahead: The EFL Championship Awaits

With Wrexham's promotion to the EFL Championship secured, the club now faces the next step in their journey. The 2024–25 season in League One will go down as one of the most significant in Wrexham's history, and their achievement of securing back-to-back promotions is a testament to the progress made under the ownership of Ryan Reynolds and Rob McElhenney.

Welcome to *Wrexham*: The Rise of the Red Dragons

As Wrexham set their sights on the Championship, they will know that the challenges will only increase, but with their solid foundation, strategic management, and unwavering fan support, the future looks incredibly bright for the Red Dragons.

Player Contributions: Key Figures in Wrexham's League One Success

In addition to the aforementioned standout performers, Wrexham's promotion to the EFL Championship was also driven by the contributions of several other players, each of whom made crucial impacts during the season. Their collective efforts ensured that Wrexham maintained their impressive form and secured another step up the football pyramid.

Sam Smith – The Emerging Goal Scorer

Sam Smith emerged as one of the standout players of the 2024–25 season, finishing as one of the club's top scorers with 18 goals in League One. His ability to find the back of the net in crucial moments made him an invaluable asset to the team. Smith's movement off the ball, his clinical finishing, and his aerial presence in the box were key factors in Wrexham's attacking success. His partnership with Paul Mullin formed a lethal attacking duo, and his development as a reliable goal-scorer will be crucial as the team moves forward to the Championship.

Ollie Rathbone – Stability and Creativity in Midfield

Ollie Rathbone played a vital role in Wrexham's midfield, contributing 8 goals over the course of the season. His dynamic style of play, coupled with his ability to control the tempo of the game, helped balance the team's attack and defense. Rathbone's intelligence on the ball, quick decision-making, and excellent passing range allowed him to dictate play and set up key attacking moves. His defensive contributions also provided the necessary stability in the middle of the park, making him an essential cog in Wrexham's promotion machine.

Steven Fletcher – Leadership and Experience Up Front

Steven Fletcher, with his wealth of experience, was a key figure in Wrexham's forward line. Scoring 8 goals in League One, Fletcher was instrumental in guiding the team through difficult matches, using his leadership and composure to influence games. His physical presence and aerial ability made him a constant threat in the box, while his work ethic and professionalism served as an example for the younger players. Fletcher's experience in high-pressure situations was invaluable, especially in games where Wrexham needed a leader to step up and drive the team forward.

Max Cleworth – Versatility and Defensive Strength

Max Cleworth enjoyed a breakout season, not only solidifying his place in the defense but also contributing 7 goals throughout the campaign. As a defender, Cleworth's strength, reading of the game, and ability to win aerial duels made him a vital part of the backline. His leadership in organizing the defense and his ability to play out from the back were crucial in maintaining Wrexham's solid defensive record. Cleworth's attacking contributions, including crucial goals from set-pieces, highlighted his versatility and his growing importance within the team.

Ryan Barnett – The Assist King

Ryan Barnett was the team's assist leader, contributing an impressive 9 assists throughout the League One season. His speed, dribbling ability, and vision made him a constant threat down the wings, while his precise crosses and key passes provided countless opportunities for his teammates. Barnett's contribution to Wrexham's attacking play was immeasurable, as he often created the final ball that led to goals. His flair and creativity made him one of the standout players in the team, and his ability to consistently provide for the strikers played a crucial role in the team's promotion.

A Collective Effort: Wrexham's Path to the EFL Championship

While individual performances were crucial to Wrexham's success in League One, it was the collective effort of the entire squad that ultimately secured the club's promotion to the EFL Championship. The strength of the team, both on and off the pitch, was a reflection of the hard work put in by all players, underpinned by strong leadership and a clear tactical plan from manager Phil Parkinson.

With a solid foundation now in place, Wrexham can look ahead to their next challenge: the EFL Championship. But with a mix of experienced heads and emerging talent, they are well-equipped to continue their upward trajectory and make their mark at the next level of English football.

Defensive Strength: A Foundation of Success

Wrexham's defense played a pivotal role in their promotion to the EFL Championship. Conceding only 34 goals across the entire 2024–25 League One season, the team boasted one of the best defensive records in the league, averaging just 0.76 goals conceded per game. The squad's ability to stay solid and resilient, even under pressure, was a direct result of their collective organization and discipline under manager Phil Parkinson.

The defensive unit's cohesion was evident through the 23 clean sheets achieved in 45 league matches, a testament to the team's ability to shut out opposition attacks and maintain focus throughout the season. Key defenders like Max Cleworth, who contributed both defensively and offensively, and experienced players like Ben Tozer, played a vital part in maintaining such a formidable defensive record.

Home and Away Form: A Balanced Approach

Wrexham's home form was crucial to their overall success. At the STōK Cae Ras, they recorded an impressive 16 wins, 5 draws, and only 2 losses. This exceptional record at home made it a fortress where the team could rely on their loyal supporters to lift them through tough matches. The atmosphere at the stadium provided an additional boost to the players, allowing them to consistently perform at their best in front of their fans.

On the road, Wrexham showed resilience, securing 10 wins, 6 draws, and 6 losses. While not as dominant as their home form, their ability to pick up points away from home further demonstrated the team's balanced approach and adaptability. These results on both fronts allowed Wrexham to maintain consistency throughout the season, a key factor in their promotion push.

Cup Competitions: Valuable Experience and Progress

While Wrexham's primary focus was securing promotion through League One, their cup run also provided important experience and insight into how they could perform against teams from higher leagues.

- **FA Cup:** Wrexham's campaign ended in disappointment as they were eliminated in the First Round. However, the early exit provided them with a chance to focus more on the league and ensure that their promotion was secured.

- **EFL Cup:** Like the FA Cup, Wrexham's run in the EFL Cup also came to an end in the First Round. The team was knocked out in the early stages, but the matches served as valuable opportunities for squad rotation and experimentation.

- **EFL Trophy:** The team's performance in the EFL Trophy was a highlight of their cup campaigns. They made it all the way to the Semi-finals, showing depth in their squad and competitive edge in knockout competitions. While they ultimately fell short of the final, their journey to the last four was an important reflection of their growing strength as a club, especially in the context of their promotion aspirations.

Wrexham's impressive defensive record, solid home and away form, and progress in cup competitions have laid a strong foundation for their next challenge in the EFL Championship. As they prepare to face tougher competition at the higher level, the lessons learned from their success in League One will be crucial. Strengthening their squad further, especially in key positions, will be vital if they are to continue their upward trajectory and remain competitive in the Championship.

Their journey from the National League to League One in such a short span is a testament to the vision, hard work, and dedication of everyone involved at the club—from the owners and management to the players and fans. Now, with the stakes higher than ever, Wrexham's story is poised to evolve even further as they take on the challenges of the EFL Championship.

Management and Ownership

Manager Phil Parkinson, appointed in 2021, continued to instill a winning mentality within the squad. His tactical acumen and leadership were instrumental in navigating the challenges of League One. Owners Ryan Reynolds and Rob McElhenney remained actively involved, providing both financial support and a global platform for the club through their media presence.

Fan Engagement: The Heart of Wrexham's Success

Wrexham's remarkable rise through the football league system was significantly fueled by the unwavering support of their fanbase. Throughout the 2024–25 season, the fans proved time and time again to be the club's greatest asset, creating an atmosphere that propelled the players forward. The fans' commitment to the club and their unmatched enthusiasm were integral to Wrexham's ability to maintain focus and consistency throughout the campaign.

The **highest attendance** recorded during the season was an impressive **13,341** spectators at the match against Shrewsbury Town on **7 September 2024**. This crowd, along with the loyal supporters who packed the stadium week after week, helped create a near-impregnable home fortress at the STōK Cae Ras.

The **average home attendance** stood at **12,795**, reflecting not only the growing popularity of the club but also the deep connection between Wrexham AFC and the local community. As the club ascended through the leagues, the fans' support remained steadfast, with the town's collective passion becoming a driving force behind Wrexham's success.

Welcome to *Wrexham*: The Rise of the Red Dragons

Conclusion: A Season of Triumph

The **2024–25 League One season** marked yet another chapter in Wrexham's storied revival under the ownership of **Ryan Reynolds and Rob McElhenney**. The club's **promotion to the EFL Championship** was a historic achievement, their third consecutive promotion, which made headlines not only in football but across the global sporting community.

This season was defined by **strategic planning**, **effective management** under **Phil Parkinson**, and **consistent performances** on the pitch. Key contributions from players like **Sam Smith**, **Ollie Rathbone**, and **Steven Fletcher** ensured that Wrexham maintained their position at the top of the league, while the defensive strength and fan support provided a solid foundation for their success.

As they now prepare to take on the challenges of the **EFL Championship**, the club's journey serves as a powerful testament to the transformative power of **vision**, **dedication**, and **community**. From their humble beginnings in the National League to the pinnacle of English football's second tier, Wrexham AFC's rise is a story of **resilience**, **hope**, and **achievement**. With the continued backing of their passionate fanbase and the leadership of their Hollywood owners, the club's future looks incredibly bright.

Championship Expectations and Prospects

Wrexham AFC's Strategic Path to Championship Stability

Wrexham AFC's incredible rise to the **EFL Championship** has been nothing short of extraordinary. Their **three consecutive**

promotions under the ownership of **Ryan Reynolds and Rob McElhenney** has captured the imagination of football fans worldwide. Now, as the club prepares for the highly competitive 2025–26 season, their focus is on **maintaining their momentum** and ensuring they are well-equipped for the challenges of the Championship.

Strategic Vision and Financial Prudence

The club's **strategic vision** is centered around **financial sustainability** while aiming for continued success on the pitch. **Executive director Humphrey Ker** has been vocal about the need to balance ambition with caution, particularly in light of the **Championship's demanding nature**. While the dream of reaching the **Premier League** remains, the club is keen on avoiding the pitfalls of reckless spending that can often jeopardize long-term stability.

Wrexham's financial approach involves **prudent investment** in both the playing squad and infrastructure, ensuring that each step taken is carefully measured. This strategy, while bold in its ambition, reflects the owners' deep understanding of the importance of **sustainability** in the modern football landscape. By setting a strong foundation off the pitch, they are positioning Wrexham for sustained success at the higher levels of English football.

Squad Development and Key Players

As the 2025–26 season approaches, **manager Phil Parkinson** remains the steady hand steering the ship. Parkinson's leadership and focus on developing a **cohesive squad** have been key factors in Wrexham's rise. While there has been speculation surrounding his future, particularly as the club adjusts to the pressures of

Welcome to *Wrexham*: The Rise of the Red Dragons

Championship football, Parkinson's experience and vision are integral to the club's strategy moving forward.

At the heart of Wrexham's attacking plans remains **Paul Mullin**, whose influence on the pitch has been immense. Despite the interest from higher-tier clubs, **Mullin** continues to be a pivotal figure for Wrexham. Both **Parkinson** and **Humphrey Ker** have expressed their confidence in the striker's ability to lead the charge, ensuring that his contributions remain central to Wrexham's attacking strategy.

Potential Signings: Leadership and Experience

In preparation for their maiden season in the **EFL Championship**, Wrexham is exploring the addition of key players to strengthen their squad. The club's focus is on **experienced players** who can offer leadership and stability without disrupting the financial principles that have guided their success thus far.

Both **Jonny Evans** and **Jamie Vardy** represent strategic signings that would offer **Wrexham AFC** a combination of **experience**, **leadership**, and **winning mentality**, vital for the club's challenge in the **EFL Championship**. Their proven pedigree at the highest level of English football, coupled with their ability to perform under pressure, makes them ideal candidates to help the team adjust to the demands of a more competitive division.

Jonny Evans

As a seasoned **central defender**, **Jonny Evans** brings a wealth of experience from his years in the Premier League with clubs like **Manchester United** and **Leicester City**. His leadership and defensive composure could provide the rock-solid foundation needed for Wrexham's backline. In addition to his physical attributes, Evans' tactical awareness and his ability to read the game would be invaluable for guiding Wrexham's younger defenders. His

Championship experience, having played for Leicester in the second tier before their rise to the Premier League, makes him a perfect fit for a club like Wrexham aiming to solidify their place in the division.

Jamie Vardy

On the other hand, **Jamie Vardy** offers a dynamic attacking threat that could elevate Wrexham's forward line. With his electrifying pace, clinical finishing, and knack for scoring crucial goals, Vardy has established himself as one of the Premier League's most formidable strikers. His remarkable rise from non-league football to the heights of the Premier League is a story that resonates with Wrexham's ethos and ambition. **Vardy's leadership** and **mentality** as a winner would also serve as a powerful influence on the younger players, encouraging them to aim higher and match his relentless pursuit of excellence.

Strategic Fit and Financial Prudence

Both players, while not at the peak of their careers, would be **wise investments** that reflect Wrexham's strategy of bringing in experienced players without jeopardizing the financial sustainability of the club. These signings would not only provide on-field benefits but also bolster the club's off-field profile as they compete at a higher level.

By signing players like Evans and Vardy, Wrexham would be sending a strong message to both fans and rivals that they are serious about establishing themselves as a **competitive force in the Championship**. At the same time, the club would be maintaining their core principles of **financial prudence**, ensuring these additions make sense in the long run.

Ultimately, the acquisition of players of such high caliber would show that **Wrexham AFC** is fully equipped to face the challenges of

Welcome to *Wrexham*: The Rise of the Red Dragons

the **EFL Championship**, while remaining true to the vision set out by their owners, **Ryan Reynolds** and **Rob McElhenney**.

The Road Ahead: Building for Long-Term Success

Wrexham AFC's journey to the **EFL Championship** is an inspiring example of how vision, ambition, and financial prudence can lead to sustained success in football. With their continued focus on **community engagement**, **strategic investments**, and **long-term stability**, the club is poised to navigate the challenges of the Championship and beyond.

As the 2025–26 season unfolds, Wrexham AFC's blend of **passionate fan support**, **prudent financial management**, and **talented squad** will be crucial in shaping their future. With the backing of their Hollywood owners and the leadership of **Phil Parkinson**, Wrexham's **ambitious climb up the football pyramid** shows no signs of slowing down. The club's success story has only just begun, and the future looks incredibly bright as they continue to chase their Premier League dream.

Infrastructure and Community Engagement

Wrexham's commitment to growth extends beyond the pitch. The development of the new Kop Stand, set to open in 2026, reflects the club's dedication to enhancing fan experience and increasing stadium capacity.

The "Welcome to Wrexham" documentary series continues to elevate the club's global profile, attracting new supporters and generating additional revenue streams. This increased visibility plays a crucial role in the club's strategic planning and community engagement efforts.

Competitive Landscape

The Championship presents a formidable challenge, featuring clubs with substantial resources and Premier League experience. Wrexham's approach focuses on leveraging their cohesive team dynamics and strategic planning to navigate this competitive landscape effectively.

As Wrexham AFC embarks on the 2025–26 Championship season, the club remains steadfast in its commitment to sustainable growth, strategic squad development, and community engagement. Balancing ambition with prudence, Wrexham aims to establish itself as a competitive force in the Championship, laying the groundwork for potential future success.

◇◇◇◇

Premier League Ambition

Ownership Vision and Commitment

The vision that **Ryan Reynolds** and **Rob McElhenney** have for **Wrexham AFC** is clear and resolute: **reaching the Premier League**. This goal, which seemed distant when they took over in 2021, is now firmly within their sights, fueled by three successive promotions and an expanding global profile. **Reynolds and McElhenney's transparency** about their aspirations has not only invigorated the club but also captured the imagination of football fans worldwide. Their belief that a club like **Wrexham**, rich in history and supported by passionate fans, has the potential to rise to the pinnacle of English football has provided both a beacon of hope for the community and a clear direction for the future. The **"Welcome to Wrexham"** documentary series has also played a crucial role in raising the club's profile, attracting new fans and investors while documenting the journey of the owners' involvement and the challenges they face in their ambitious pursuit.

Financial Strategy and Sustainability

While the Premier League dream is an exciting proposition, the road to achieving it requires careful planning, financial acumen, and sustainable growth. Under the leadership of **Humphrey Ker**, Wrexham AFC is adopting a **strategic financial approach** to ensure that their rise through the ranks is not hindered by fiscal mismanagement. As the club enters the **EFL Championship**—a highly competitive league with vastly different financial dynamics—there will be significant challenges. Many of the clubs in this division benefit from the **Premier League parachute payments**, which give them a financial cushion after relegation, making the fight for promotion even more difficult.

However, Wrexham's owners have been clear in their intent to balance ambition with **financial sustainability**. The club's **reported £26.7 million revenue in 2023–24** showcases the potential for growth, particularly in terms of matchday income, sponsorships, and global exposure. The challenge now lies in using this increased revenue wisely—investing in the squad, infrastructure, and facilities while keeping an eye on the long-term financial health of the club. Wrexham's ambition to **reach the Premier League** doesn't mean reckless spending but rather making strategic investments that will allow them to compete at the highest level without jeopardizing the club's financial future.

Challenges Ahead

As Wrexham steps into the **EFL Championship** in the 2025–26 season, they will face several challenges. The gap in quality, experience, and resources between the Championship and League One is considerable. Clubs in the Championship often have larger budgets, higher-caliber players, and the luxury of more extensive scouting networks. For Wrexham, competing on such a level will require a combination of smart player recruitment, effective squad management, and the development of a playing style that can withstand the intensity of the division.

Another challenge is the **competition for promotion**. Only two teams can secure automatic promotion to the Premier League each season, and with the financial rewards and prestige at stake, the competition is fierce. Wrexham will need to find a way to bridge the gap between **League One** and the **Premier League**, which often means looking for **under-valued gems** in the transfer market and developing young talent that can make an immediate impact.

Strategic Investments and Squad Development

As part of their strategy to secure promotion, Wrexham will continue to focus on **strengthening their squad** and enhancing the quality of their play. The club's ownership has indicated that they will be targeting both **experienced players** with Championship-level pedigree and **promising young talents** to develop over time. This dual approach is intended to balance the immediate needs of the squad with the long-term goal of building a team capable of competing in the **Premier League**.

The club has already made strides in strengthening its squad, with **Paul Mullin** emerging as a key figure in attack, while the addition of experienced defenders like **Jonny Evans** and **midfielders like Ollie Rathbone** have added valuable depth. The emphasis on bringing in **Premier League-caliber players** or those with substantial experience in the Championship would allow Wrexham to accelerate their transition to the highest tier of English football. Furthermore, the ownership is keen on fostering a winning **mentality**, with players who understand the pressures and demands of promotion.

Welcome to *Wrexham*: The Rise of the Red Dragons

The Premier League Dream

While Wrexham AFC has made significant progress in recent years, the road to the **Premier League** remains a long and challenging one. However, with the backing of **Ryan Reynolds** and **Rob McElhenney**, a solid financial strategy, and the drive to develop a competitive team, the club is poised to continue its rise. Their ambitions are more than just a pipe dream; they are grounded in practical steps that will help Wrexham establish itself as a **mainstay in the Championship** and, eventually, make a push for promotion to the Premier League.

The journey ahead will undoubtedly test the club's resolve and resilience, but the **Wrexham AFC story** is one of **overcoming obstacles**, believing in the impossible, and making that dream a reality—both for the club's owners and the **loyal fans** who have supported the team through thick and thin. The next chapter in Wrexham's saga is set to be written in the high stakes world of the **EFL Championship**, with their sights firmly set on the **Premier League**.

Recruitment Philosophy

Manager **Phil Parkinson** has implemented a **recruitment policy** at Wrexham AFC that places a strong emphasis on **team cohesion** and **character**. Rather than chasing high-profile signings or players with big reputations, Parkinson has focused on bringing in individuals who fit the **club's culture** and **values**. This approach, centered around the mantra of **"no superstars and no egos,"** has been instrumental in fostering a unified and resilient squad—key components of Wrexham's recent successes.

Wrexham's rise through the leagues has been built on the strength of **teamwork** rather than individual brilliance. Each player is expected to understand their role within the squad, contribute to the collective effort, and fit seamlessly into a group dynamic where humility and hard work are paramount. This philosophy is aligned with

Parkinson's desire to create a squad that is greater than the sum of its parts—a team that excels due to **solidarity** and **mutual respect**, rather than relying on any one individual to carry the load.

While there is always room for high-quality talent, Parkinson's strategy ensures that **character** is just as important as technical ability. Players who display strong leadership, resilience, and a willingness to work for the team are prioritized. This has allowed Wrexham to maintain a harmonious atmosphere within the dressing room, which is crucial in a competitive environment like the **EFL Championship**.

This **recruitment philosophy** not only strengthens the **team dynamic** but also reinforces Wrexham's **club ethos**. The **no egos** approach fosters a sense of unity and shared responsibility, helping to keep everyone grounded despite the club's rising profile. As Wrexham continues their climb through the football pyramid, this commitment to **team-first values** will serve as a critical foundation in their pursuit of higher honors, including a potential place in the **Premier League**.

Infrastructure Development

To support their Premier League aspirations, Wrexham is investing in infrastructure improvements, including the development of the new Kop Stand, set to open in 2026. These enhancements are designed to increase stadium capacity and improve facilities, thereby boosting matchday revenues and enhancing the fan experience.

Competitive Landscape

The Championship presents a formidable challenge, with numerous clubs vying for promotion. The presence of recently relegated Premier League teams with substantial resources underscores the competitiveness of the league. Wrexham's strategy involves meticulous planning and leveraging their unique global profile to attract talent and investment.

Wrexham AFC's journey toward the Premier League is characterized by ambitious yet measured steps. The club's leadership remains steadfast in their vision, balancing aspiration with sustainability. As they navigate the challenges of the Championship, Wrexham continues to embody a model of strategic growth and community engagement, keeping the dream of Premier League football within reach.

FA Cup Performance and Analysis

The **2024–25 FA Cup** campaign for **Wrexham AFC** was a short-lived affair, ending with a **first-round exit** after a disappointing 1–0 defeat to **Harrogate Town**. This chapter delves into the specifics of the match, the tactical approaches employed by both teams, and the wider implications for Wrexham's season and future cup performances.

Welcome to *Wrexham*: The Rise of the Red Dragons

Match Overview

- **Fixture:** Harrogate Town vs. Wrexham AFC
- **Date:** 3 November 2024
- **Venue:** EnviroVent Stadium
- **Result:** Harrogate Town 1–0 Wrexham AFC

Wrexham's **FA Cup** journey came to an abrupt halt with a **1–0 defeat** away to **Harrogate Town**. The match saw Wrexham struggle to break down a well-organized Harrogate defense, with the only goal of the game coming from **Jack Muldoon** in the 24th minute. Despite their efforts to equalize in the second half, **Wrexham** could not penetrate the resolute **Harrogate defense**, and their cup run ended at the **first-round stage**.

Tactical Analysis

Wrexham approached the match with a **4-3-3 formation** that sought to control possession in midfield and utilize their wingers in wide areas. Manager **Phil Parkinson** had clearly instructed his side to dictate the tempo and press high up the pitch to force mistakes from the opposition. However, **Harrogate Town** executed a tactical approach that stifled Wrexham's fluid attacking game.

- **Harrogate's Defensive Setup:**
  Harrogate deployed a **compact defensive block** designed to close down space in central areas and limit the attacking influence of Wrexham's midfield. Their midfielders worked tirelessly to **press Wrexham's creative players**, preventing them from finding the rhythm that has characterized their recent successes in the league. As a result, Wrexham struggled to break through Harrogate's lines and found themselves forced to play **long balls** or take speculative shots from range.

Welcome to *Wrexham*: The Rise of the Red Dragons

- **The Early Goal and Tactical Adjustments:**
  Wrexham's task was made more difficult when Harrogate
  took the lead in the 24th minute. The early goal forced
  Wrexham into a more attacking posture, increasing their risk-
  taking and leaving them vulnerable to counter-attacks.
  Parkinson responded by making **early substitutions**,
  introducing fresh legs to provide **pace and creativity**, with
  the hope of finding an equalizer.

- **Wrexham's Offensive Struggles:**
  Despite the tactical changes, Wrexham was unable to break
  down Harrogate's disciplined defense. Their **set-piece
  efforts**—which had been a key source of goals in their league
  campaign—failed to find their mark. Likewise, **long-range
  efforts** from **Paul Mullin** and others were easily dealt with
  by **Harrogate's goalkeeper** and defense. The lack of **cutting
  edge** in the final third highlighted Wrexham's inability to
  adapt to Harrogate's defensive strategy.

Implications for the Club's Broader Objectives

The **FA Cup** exit marked a disappointing result for Wrexham,
especially given the **club's ambition** to make a mark in cup
competitions alongside their league performances. While the loss did
not detract from their **League One campaign**, it underscored some
tactical shortcomings that could be addressed moving forward.

- **Cup Focus vs. League Priorities:**
  The first-round exit, while disappointing, could serve as a
  valuable learning experience for both the coaching staff and
  players. With **promotion to the Championship** on the
  horizon, the **FA Cup** may not have been the priority for
  Wrexham in the grand scheme of the season. However, this
  loss serves as a reminder that consistent preparation and

tactical flexibility are required to compete on multiple fronts.

- **Future Cup Competitions:**
Looking ahead, Wrexham's **focus on cup competitions** will likely need to be more intense, with a greater emphasis on **depth in the squad** and **adaptability in tactics**. The defeat to Harrogate highlighted that while the team can dominate in league fixtures, they must adapt their approach in knockout games where one-off performances are crucial. Going forward, improving their ability to break down defensively-minded sides will be key to advancing in future cups.

The 1–0 defeat to Harrogate Town in the **2024–25 FA Cup** first round was a disappointing result for Wrexham AFC, but it offered valuable lessons for the club as they prepare for life in **League One**. While the FA Cup is important, Wrexham's priority must remain on league success and building a squad capable of competing at the highest level. This loss should not detract from the club's overall progress; instead, it should be seen as an opportunity to reflect, learn, and improve for the future.

Player Performances

- **Arthur Okonkwo (Goalkeeper)**: Demonstrated composure and made crucial saves to keep Wrexham in contention.

- **George Dobson (Midfielder)**: Showed tenacity in midfield battles but struggled to create significant chances.

- **Paul Mullin (Forward)**: Worked tirelessly upfront but was effectively marked by Harrogate's defenders, limiting his impact.

Implications and Reflections

The early exit from the FA Cup was a disappointment for Wrexham, especially considering their aspirations to test themselves against higher-tier opposition. However, this outcome allowed the team to focus resources and energy on their League One campaign, which ultimately resulted in promotion to the Championship.

Manager Phil Parkinson acknowledged the setback but emphasized the importance of learning from the experience. He highlighted the need for adaptability and resilience in knockout competitions, where single-match dynamics can differ significantly from league play.

While the 2024–25 FA Cup journey was short-lived for Wrexham AFC, it provided valuable insights into areas requiring improvement, particularly in adapting tactics against defensively robust teams. The experience underscored the unpredictability of cup competitions and the necessity for strategic flexibility.

The Kop Stand   A Symbol of Wrexham s Revival

The redevelopment of the Kop Stand at Wrexham AFC's STōK Cae Ras stadium represents a significant milestone in the club's ongoing transformation. This chapter provides a comprehensive overview of the project's inception, design, and anticipated impact on the club and its supporters.

Welcome to *Wrexham*: The Rise of the Red Dragons

Historical Context

The Kop Stand, historically known as the Crispin Lane End or "Town End," has been an integral part of Wrexham's football heritage. Named after the Battle of Spion Kop, it was once the largest all-standing terrace in the English Football League, accommodating up to 5,000 spectators. However, due to safety concerns, it was closed in 2008 and remained unused for several years. In January 2023, the stand was demolished to pave the way for a modern redevelopment.

Redevelopment Plans

Capacity and Compliance

The new Kop Stand is designed to accommodate 5,500 spectators, including provisions for safe standing, hospitality suites, and accessible seating. This redevelopment aims to bring the stadium up to UEFA Category 4 standards, enabling it to host international events such as the UEFA European Under-19 Championship finals in 2026.

Architectural Design

Renowned architectural firm Populous has been commissioned to lead the design of the new stand. The structure will feature a distinctive red brick façade, paying homage to Wrexham's nickname, "Terracottapolis," and incorporating elements that reflect the town's industrial heritage. Two dragons, emblematic of the club's crest, will adorn the exterior, symbolizing strength and unity.

Acoustic Enhancements

The design includes a roof structure engineered to amplify crowd noise, creating an intimidating atmosphere for visiting teams and enhancing the matchday experience for supporters. This focus on acoustics aims to reestablish the Kop Stand as the heart of fan engagement within the stadium.

Temporary Measures

To accommodate fans during the redevelopment, a temporary stand was installed at the Kop End in December 2023. This structure provides seating for 2,309 supporters, including 20 wheelchair-accessible spaces. While not fully enclosed, it offers an interim solution to maintain stadium capacity during construction.

Community and Economic Impact

The Kop Stand redevelopment is a central component of the broader Wrexham Gateway project, which includes plans for new office spaces and improved infrastructure in the surrounding area. These developments are expected to stimulate local economic growth and enhance the town's appeal as a destination for sports and tourism.

Financial Considerations

The project aligns with Wrexham AFC's commitment to financial sustainability. Despite significant investments in infrastructure and squad development, the club has reported a record turnover of £26.7 million for the year ending June 30, 2024, reflecting a 155% increase from the previous year. This financial growth underscores the club's strategic approach to balancing ambition with fiscal responsibility.

Future Outlook

The completion of the new Kop Stand is anticipated in time for the 2026/27 season, coinciding with the club's aspirations to solidify its position in the Championship and potentially secure promotion to the Premier League. The enhanced facilities are expected to bolster matchday revenues, attract higher-caliber players, and provide a platform for sustained success on and off the pitch.

The redevelopment of the Kop Stand signifies more than just a structural upgrade; it embodies Wrexham AFC's resurgence and the community's renewed sense of pride and optimism. As the club continues its upward trajectory, the new stand will serve as a testament to the enduring spirit of Wrexham and its supporters.

Chapter 11: Coaching Staff and Performance Analysis

Wrexham AFC's meteoric rise through the English football leagues has been underpinned by a cohesive and strategic coaching framework. This chapter delves into the composition of the coaching staff, their methodologies, and the impact they've had on the club's recent successes.

1. Leadership at the Helm: Phil Parkinson

Appointed in July 2021, Phil Parkinson brought a wealth of experience to Wrexham, having managed clubs like Colchester United, Hull City, and Bradford City. His pragmatic approach and emphasis on team cohesion have been instrumental in Wrexham's consecutive promotions. Parkinson's philosophy centers on building a resilient squad, focusing on character and unity over individual flair. He has consistently highlighted the importance of maintaining the club's culture, avoiding the pitfalls of star-centric team dynamics. Under his guidance, Wrexham has achieved a historic ascent, moving from the National League to the Championship in just three seasons.

2. Assistant Coaching and Support Staff

While specific details about the assistant coaching staff are limited, it's evident that Parkinson's team operates with a clear division of responsibilities, ensuring comprehensive coverage of all aspects of player development and match preparation. The collaborative environment fosters continuous improvement, with each member contributing to the club's overarching goals.

3. Tactical Evolution and Match Preparation

Parkinson's tactical acumen is evident in Wrexham's adaptability on the pitch. The team has demonstrated versatility, adjusting formations and strategies to counter various opponents effectively. A notable aspect of their play has been the emphasis on set-pieces, with the team capitalizing on these opportunities to secure crucial goals. This focus on maximizing every facet of the game underscores the coaching staff's meticulous preparation and attention to detail.

4. Player Development and Squad Rotation

The coaching staff has shown a keen eye for talent development, nurturing players to reach their potential. Strategic squad rotation has been employed to maintain player fitness and morale, ensuring that the team remains competitive throughout the grueling football season. This approach has also allowed emerging talents to gain valuable experience, contributing to the team's depth and resilience.

5. Emphasis on Mental Fortitude

As Wrexham AFC continues to ascend through the English football pyramid, **mental fortitude** has become a cornerstone of their overall development. While physical fitness and tactical awareness are vital, the psychological demands of competing at higher levels, particularly in **high-stakes matches** and under the pressure of rapid promotion, cannot be overlooked.

The Role of Mental Strength in High-Stakes Matches

The challenges that accompany promotion—where expectations are higher, and every match feels more critical—can often create **psychological stress** for players. The club's coaching staff, under **Phil Parkinson**, has recognized this and placed a significant focus on preparing players mentally for the intense demands of competition. These high-pressure environments require players to remain **calm under pressure**, **stay focused on their tasks**, and **resist distractions** from external pressures, including the intense scrutiny that comes with Wrexham's growing profile.

Supporting Players' Mental Well-Being

In addition to physical training, the club has adopted a holistic approach, incorporating **mental health support**, **stress management techniques**, and **resilience training** into their weekly routines. This emphasis on mental strength is a vital component of Wrexham's continued success, as players are not only asked to perform physically but also to **maintain emotional balance** during the most challenging moments.

Some key initiatives include:

- **Sports Psychology Support**: The inclusion of a dedicated sports psychologist who works closely with the players to address issues such as **performance anxiety**, **mental fatigue**, and **confidence-building**. This allows players to cope effectively with the pressures of big games and helps them approach each match with a positive mindset.

- **Team-Building Activities**: The coaching staff also organizes activities that focus on **team bonding** and **mental conditioning**. These activities are designed to foster a sense of unity among the squad, build trust, and enhance

> collaboration both on and off the pitch. Strong team dynamics often improve performance, particularly in high-pressure situations where cohesion can make all the difference.

- **Individual Mental Coaching**: Recognizing that each player has unique psychological needs, the club offers individualized mental coaching tailored to help each player cope with their personal challenges, whether that be handling injuries, adjusting to new team roles, or adapting to the competitive environment in **League One**.

Building Mental Resilience for Long-Term Success

As Wrexham transitions into the **Championship** and continues to dream of reaching the **Premier League**, mental resilience will be more important than ever. The club's focus on mental fortitude is not a temporary measure but a long-term strategy. Players need to be **mentally prepared** to cope with setbacks, such as defeats or injuries, and still perform at their best in the next match. By fostering a mentally resilient squad, the club aims to build not only a **physically talented team** but also a **psychologically strong** one, capable of handling the highs and lows of elite football.

This psychological preparation is critical in shaping a **winning mindset**—one that remains focused on goals, fights through adversity, and maintains the club's **ambition to reach the Premier League**. Ultimately, mental fortitude will play a key role in **sustaining success** at the highest levels of competition.

By investing in both the physical and mental well-being of its players, Wrexham AFC has created a balanced approach to development that addresses the many challenges of competitive football. This focus on **mental strength** ensures that the club will be well-equipped to handle the pressures of their future journey in the **Championship** and beyond.

6. Integration of Sports Science

In the modern era of football, the integration of **sports science** into training regimens is no longer optional but essential. Wrexham AFC has fully embraced this approach, incorporating **advanced data analytics**, **injury prevention techniques**, and **recovery strategies** into their day-to-day operations. This scientific approach, combined with traditional coaching methods, has provided a comprehensive framework for player development, **performance optimization**, and long-term **player welfare**.

Data-Driven Performance Monitoring

One of the key components of Wrexham's approach is the use of **data analytics** to track player performance. Through advanced performance metrics, such as **distance covered**, **sprinting speeds**, **heart rate zones**, and **acceleration data**, the coaching staff can gain detailed insights into how players are performing during training and matches.

- **Real-Time Monitoring**: During matches and training sessions, **wearable technology**, such as **GPS trackers** and **heart rate monitors**, allows the coaching staff to track player movement, effort levels, and fatigue in real-time. This data helps coaches make informed decisions about player substitutions, rotation, and overall workload management, reducing the risk of **overtraining** and **fatigue-related injuries**.

- **Post-Match Analytics**: After matches, the team uses data to assess **tactical effectiveness**, individual player contributions, and areas for improvement. This includes reviewing aspects such as **possession stats**, **passing accuracy**, **shots on goal**, and **defensive actions** to identify both strengths and weaknesses in the team's performance. Players then receive personalized feedback to refine their skills.

Injury Prevention and Recovery

The demands of professional football can take a significant toll on players' bodies. To mitigate the risk of injuries and aid recovery, Wrexham has incorporated **sports science-based injury prevention** and recovery protocols into their regimen.

- **Prehabilitation Programs**: These exercises focus on **strengthening muscles** and improving **flexibility** to prevent common injuries such as **hamstring strains** or **ankle sprains**. By targeting areas that are particularly vulnerable to injury, such as the lower back, knees, and hips, the club can reduce the likelihood of players suffering setbacks that could impact their performance.

- **Biomechanical Analysis**: Wrexham employs **motion capture technology** and **video analysis** to assess players' movements and detect any potential flaws in their techniques that could lead to injury. Adjustments are made to **improve posture**, **movement efficiency**, and **gait patterns**, ensuring that players perform at their best while minimizing risk.

- **Recovery Protocols**: Recovery is equally important, and Wrexham has adopted **state-of-the-art recovery technologies** such as **cryotherapy**, **hydrotherapy**, and **physiotherapy** to help players recover faster after intense training sessions or matches. The use of **cold-water immersion** helps reduce muscle inflammation, while **stretching** and **massage therapy** are incorporated to alleviate muscle tightness and improve flexibility.

- **Sleep and Nutrition Monitoring**: Wrexham's sports science team also monitors **sleep patterns** and **nutrition** to ensure that players are fully rested and fueled for optimal performance. Data from sleep trackers and food diaries help to personalize **sleep management** and **dietary plans**, promoting recovery and energy levels.

Sports Science and Mental Wellness

The integration of **sports science** extends beyond physical aspects. Wrexham recognizes the link between **mental health** and physical performance. As such, the club works closely with **sports psychologists** to ensure that players not only recover physically but are also mentally prepared for the challenges of professional football.

- **Mindfulness Techniques**: Coaches and staff introduce players to mindfulness practices, which help them manage stress, stay focused during matches, and recover mentally after tough performances.

- **Mental Resilience Training**: Wrexham's coaching team integrates **mental resilience exercises** into training, allowing players to stay calm under pressure, recover from mistakes, and continue to perform at their best during critical moments in matches.

Long-Term Player Development

By using data analytics and sports science in tandem with traditional coaching methods, Wrexham AFC has developed a **holistic approach** to player development. This not only enhances the team's immediate performance but also ensures the long-term health and sustainability of the players' careers.

- **Youth Development**: As the club continues to invest in its youth academy, sports science will play an integral role in the development of younger players, helping them to avoid injury and reach their full potential through tailored training and recovery plans.

Welcome to *Wrexham*: The Rise of the Red Dragons

Wrexham AFC's commitment to integrating **sports science** into their operations underscores the club's ambition to compete at the highest levels of English football. By combining cutting-edge technology, injury prevention strategies, and a focus on overall player well-being, Wrexham has created a foundation that allows for **maximum performance** while safeguarding the future of its players. This scientific approach will be vital as the club looks to continue its rise through the **Championship** and ultimately strive for **Premier League** status.

7. Community Engagement and Club Culture

The coaching staff, led by Parkinson, has been instrumental in fostering a strong connection between the club and its supporters. By engaging with the community and upholding the club's traditions, they've cultivated a sense of unity and pride. This bond has been a driving force behind the team's motivation and has galvanized fan support during pivotal moments.

8. Challenges and Adaptations

Transitioning through the leagues presents unique challenges, from facing more formidable opponents to adapting to different styles of play. The coaching staff has navigated these transitions adeptly, continuously refining tactics and training methodologies to meet the evolving demands of higher-tier football.

9. Future Outlook

As Wrexham prepares for its campaign in the Championship, the coaching staff's role becomes even more critical. Their ability to adapt, innovate, and inspire will be paramount in ensuring the club not only survives but thrives in the highly competitive environment of the second tier.

In conclusion, Wrexham AFC's coaching staff, under the leadership of Phil Parkinson, has been a cornerstone of the club's recent achievements. Their strategic vision, commitment to player development, and deep connection with the club's ethos have set the foundation for continued success.

Home Matches Performance and Analysis

Wrexham AFC's 2024–25 season at the Racecourse Ground was marked by exceptional home performances, playing a pivotal role in their historic promotion to the EFL Championship. This chapter provides a comprehensive analysis of their home match statistics, key fixtures, and the tactical strategies that underpinned their success.

1. Overall Home Record

- **Total Home Matches**: 23
- **Wins**: 16
- **Draws**: 5
- **Losses**: 2

Welcome to *Wrexham*: The Rise of the Red Dragons

- **Win Percentage**: 70%

- **Points Per Game**: 2.30

- **Goals Scored per Game**: 1.78

- **Goals Conceded per Game**: 0.65

- **Clean Sheets**: 57%

- **Failed to Score**: 9%

- **Won to Nil**: 48%

- **Lost to Nil**: 0%

Wrexham's formidable home record was characterized by a high win rate and a strong defensive foundation, conceding less than a goal per game on average. The team maintained an impressive clean sheet percentage, reflecting their defensive solidity at the Racecourse Ground.

2. Key Home Fixtures

The **2024–25 season** was a defining one for **Wrexham AFC**, with several standout home performances playing a critical role in securing their **promotion to the Championship**. These fixtures were not only vital in terms of securing points but also in boosting the team's morale and proving their capabilities on the home front.

1. Wrexham 3–0 Reading (24 August 2024)

- **Match Overview**: From the very beginning of the season, Wrexham showed their attacking intent with a dominant 3–0 victory over **Reading** at home. This performance set the tone for what was to come, with the team demonstrating exceptional offensive coordination and tactical fluidity.

- **Key Moment**: Early goals gave the team a solid foundation, and despite Reading's attempts to mount a comeback,

Wrexham's defense remained resolute. The performance showcased their ambition to compete at the higher level of League One.

2. Wrexham 4–1 Northampton (5 October 2024)

- **Match Overview**: A resounding 4–1 victory over **Northampton** marked one of Wrexham's most comprehensive wins of the season. The attacking trio proved clinical, making quick work of Northampton's defense and solidifying Wrexham's position as a serious contender for promotion.

- **Key Moment**: A first-half hat-trick from **Sam Smith** demonstrated his goal-scoring prowess and confirmed his status as one of the league's top strikers. The team's ability to dominate such a competitive side was a clear sign of their growing confidence.

3. Wrexham 3–0 Exeter (23 November 2024)

- **Match Overview**: The game against **Exeter** was a well-rounded performance, combining solid defense with effective offensive transitions. The 3–0 win served as a statement of intent, with Wrexham reinforcing their credentials as one of the league's top sides.

- **Key Moment**: A stunning long-range strike from **Ryan Barnett** set the tone early in the match, and the team's subsequent goals showcased their ability to capitalize on key moments. The game also highlighted the depth of the squad, with contributions from players across the pitch.

4. Wrexham 3–0 Burton Albion (5 April 2025)

- **Match Overview**: As the season entered its final stretch, **Wrexham's 3–0 victory over Burton Albion** was crucial in keeping their promotion hopes alive. A late-season win like

> this demonstrated the resilience of the squad and their ability to handle the pressure of the promotion race.

- **Key Moment**: With the scoreline tied at 0–0 heading into the second half, the team displayed a composed and clinical approach to secure all three points, setting the stage for their push to secure promotion in the final weeks.

5. Wrexham 3–0 Charlton Athletic (26 April 2025)

- **Match Overview**: This was the moment when **Wrexham AFC** secured their **promotion to the Championship** with a commanding 3–0 victory over **Charlton Athletic**. The win not only confirmed their status as one of the best teams in League One but also capped off a remarkable run that saw them push for automatic promotion.

- **Key Moment**: The decisive victory came courtesy of **Steven Fletcher's** leadership and timely goals, alongside a solid defensive display. The moment that saw **Wrexham** secure their place in the **Championship** was met with jubilant celebrations, both on the pitch and in the stands.

These key home fixtures were not just results; they were building blocks that contributed to Wrexham's ascent to the **EFL Championship**. With each dominant win, the team gained more confidence, more momentum, and more belief in their abilities. The home form at **STōK Cae Ras** was instrumental in their journey, showcasing the unity, tactical efficiency, and ambition that became the hallmark of **Wrexham AFC's** successful 2024–25 campaign.

3. Tactical Approach at Home

Manager Phil Parkinson employed a proactive and aggressive tactical approach during home matches. The team often utilized a high-pressing system to disrupt opponents' build-up play, coupled with quick transitions to exploit defensive gaps. Set-pieces were a notable strength, with Wrexham capitalizing on corners and free-kicks to create scoring opportunities.

The midfield trio provided stability and control, allowing full-backs to advance and support attacks, thereby creating numerical advantages in wide areas. This strategy facilitated a dynamic and fluid offensive structure, overwhelming visiting teams.

4. Fan Support and Atmosphere

The passionate fanbase at the Racecourse Ground played a vital role in Wrexham's home success. The electrifying atmosphere generated by supporters created an intimidating environment for visiting teams and served as a catalyst for the players' spirited performances. The synergy between the team and its fans was evident throughout the season, culminating in jubilant celebrations following the promotion-clinching victory against Charlton Athletic.

5. Comparative Analysis

When compared to league averages, Wrexham's home performance metrics were superior across multiple categories:

- **Win Percentage**: Wrexham 70% vs. League Average 43%

- **Goals Scored per Game**: Wrexham 1.78 vs. League Average 1.40

- **Goals Conceded per Game**: Wrexham 0.65 vs. League Average 1.17

- **Clean Sheets**: Wrexham 57% vs. League Average 31%

These statistics underscore Wrexham's dominance at home and their tactical efficiency in both offensive and defensive phases.

Welcome to *Wrexham*: The Rise of the Red Dragons

Wrexham AFC's exceptional home performances during the 2024–25 season were a cornerstone of their historic promotion to the EFL Championship. The combination of strategic tactical planning, robust defensive organization, and fervent fan support created a formidable home advantage. As the club prepares for the challenges of the Championship, maintaining this home fortress will be crucial to their continued success.

◇◇◇◇

Away Matches Performance and Analysis

Wrexham AFC's 2024–25 season was not only defined by their dominant home form but also by their resilience and tactical discipline in away matches. Their ability to secure valuable points on the road played a pivotal role in their promotion to the **EFL Championship**. This chapter delves into the statistics, key fixtures, and tactical analysis of Wrexham's away matches.

1. Overall Away Record

- **Total Away Matches**: 22
- **Wins**: 10
- **Draws**: 6
- **Losses**: 6
- **Goals Scored**: 24
- **Goals Conceded**: 19

- **Goal Difference**: +5

- **Points Accumulated**: 36

Wrexham's away record was a key contributor to their overall success. With a win rate of 45% and an average of **1.64 points per game**, their away form exceeded expectations. This performance was particularly notable in a competitive league like **League One**, where teams often struggle to maintain consistency on the road. Their ability to take points from tough away games was crucial in securing the **automatic promotion** that they had worked so hard to achieve.

2. Key Away Fixtures

Wrexham 2–1 Sheffield Wednesday (13 September 2024)

- **Match Overview**: Wrexham secured an impressive 2–1 victory over **Sheffield Wednesday** at Hillsborough, one of the league's most challenging venues. The match was a testament to Wrexham's ability to fight for every point, as they overcame a strong opposition with grit and determination.

- **Key Moment**: A stunning header from **Steven Fletcher** gave Wrexham the lead, and despite a late push from Sheffield Wednesday, they held firm to secure the victory. The match epitomized their resilience and ability to perform under pressure.

Wrexham 1–1 Ipswich Town (17 November 2024)

- **Match Overview**: A hard-fought draw away at **Ipswich Town** demonstrated Wrexham's ability to manage difficult games and take points from high-caliber teams. The 1–1 draw showed the team's ability to adapt to varying styles of play and remain competitive even in hostile environments.

- **Key Moment**: A late equalizer from **Ollie Rathbone** ensured Wrexham left Portman Road with a valuable point. The performance highlighted their tactical maturity and mental fortitude to stay in the game until the final whistle.

Wrexham 3–2 Oxford United (1 December 2024)

- **Match Overview**: A thrilling 3–2 win over **Oxford United** on the road saw Wrexham outlast their opponents in a back-and-forth encounter. The attacking flair displayed in this fixture was one of the season's most memorable.

- **Key Moment**: **Max Cleworth** scored a crucial goal from a set-piece, and **Sam Smith's** clinical finish sealed the win. This match showcased the attacking potency and set-piece expertise that Wrexham had developed throughout the season.

Wrexham 0–1 Derby County (21 January 2025)

- **Match Overview**: Although **Wrexham** suffered a narrow 1–0 defeat at **Derby County**, the performance showed their defensive organization and resilience. While unable to secure a point, the match reinforced the team's capacity to compete against one of the stronger teams in the league.

- **Key Moment**: The only goal came from a mistake in Wrexham's defensive third, but despite the loss, Wrexham held their own and created several chances, indicating their potential against tough opposition.

Wrexham 2–0 Portsmouth (15 March 2025)

- **Match Overview**: A dominant 2–0 victory over **Portsmouth** on the road was another statement win, further solidifying Wrexham's credentials as serious contenders for promotion. This match demonstrated the team's growing tactical maturity and ability to control the game away from home.

- **Key Moment**: **Ryan Barnett** and **Paul Mullin** scored the goals that sealed the victory. The match also saw Wrexham's defense put in a strong performance, neutralizing Portsmouth's attacking threats.

3. Tactical Analysis of Away Form

- **Defensive Solidity**: One of the key aspects of Wrexham's success away from home was their defensive solidity. Conceding only **19 goals** in **22 away matches** meant that they were difficult to break down, even in challenging environments. The defense, led by **Max Cleworth** and **Ben Tozer**, was well-drilled and showed an impressive ability to absorb pressure.

- **Counter-Attacking Play**: Wrexham's counter-attacking style proved particularly effective away from home. With **Ryan Barnett** and **Ollie Rathbone** using their pace and creativity to exploit opposition weaknesses on the break, Wrexham were able to capitalize on mistakes and quick transitions. Their ability to strike with precision when given space was evident in key matches.

- **Midfield Control**: Away matches often presented challenges in midfield, but Wrexham's central midfielders, including **Ollie Rathbone** and **Jordan Davies**, played pivotal roles in dictating the tempo of games. Their ability to break up opposition attacks and control possession was critical in away victories, especially in tough, high-pressure games.

- **Set-Piece Threat**: Wrexham's proficiency in set-pieces, both defensively and offensively, was a recurring theme in their away fixtures. Goals from **Max Cleworth** and other defenders from corners and free-kicks played a significant role in their ability to grind out wins, especially in tightly contested matches.

4. Away Challenges and Areas for Improvement

Despite a strong away record, there were challenges that Wrexham faced throughout the season on the road. The team struggled in a few fixtures against top-tier Championship sides, where the opposition's experience in handling high-pressure games made a difference. Improving their consistency in those types of games will be crucial as they prepare for their **Championship** debut in the 2025–26 season.

Wrexham AFC's away form in the **2024–25 season** was a vital component of their promotion push. With a total of **36 points** secured on the road, their ability to perform in difficult conditions and manage high-pressure situations on away trips was central to their success. Moving forward into the **Championship**, continuing this strong away form will be key to their aspirations of further progression up the football pyramid. The balance between solid defensive structures, quick counter-attacks, and midfield control will be essential to competing at the highest level.

2. Key Away Fixtures

- **Peterborough 0–2 Wrexham (31 August 2024)**: A statement victory early in the season, showcasing Wrexham's defensive solidity and clinical finishing.

- **Rotherham 0–1 Wrexham (19 October 2024)**: A hard-fought win demonstrating resilience and tactical discipline.

- **Wycombe 0–1 Wrexham (15 March 2025)**: A crucial late-season victory against promotion rivals, highlighting Wrexham's ability to perform under pressure.

- **Exeter 0–2 Wrexham (29 March 2025)**: An emphatic win that reinforced their promotion credentials.

- **Blackpool 1–2 Wrexham (21 April 2025)**: A significant result in the final stages of the season, underlining their consistency away from home.

3. Tactical Approach in Away Matches

Manager Phil Parkinson adopted a pragmatic and adaptable tactical approach for away fixtures. The team often employed a compact defensive structure, focusing on maintaining shape and limiting the opposition's space. Quick transitions and counter-attacks were utilized to exploit opponents' vulnerabilities, with emphasis on set-pieces and capitalizing on scoring opportunities.

4. Defensive Resilience

- **Goals Conceded per Game**: 0.86

- **Clean Sheets**: 45% of away matches

- **Lead-Defending Rate**: 59%

- Wrexham's defensive organization was a cornerstone of their away success, with a goals conceded per game ratio significantly lower than the league average of 1.40. Their ability to maintain leads and secure clean sheets was indicative of their disciplined defensive performances.

5. Offensive Efficiency

- **Goals Scored per Game**: 1.09

- **Scored First in Matches**: 64%

- **Points per Game when Scoring First**: 2.71

While not the highest-scoring team away from home, Wrexham's efficiency in converting chances and securing points when scoring first was notable. Their ability to take early leads and manage games effectively contributed to their strong away record.

6. Comparative Analysis

Compared to league averages, Wrexham's away performance metrics were superior in several key areas:

- **Win Percentage**: 45% (League Average: 33%)
- **Goals Conceded per Game**: 0.86 (League Average: 1.40)
- **Clean Sheets**: 45% (League Average: 27%)
- **Points per Game**: 1.64 (League Average: 1.22)

These statistics underscore Wrexham's effectiveness and consistency in away fixtures, setting them apart from many of their competitors.

7. Challenges and Adaptations

Throughout the season, Wrexham faced various challenges in away matches, including injuries, suspensions, and tactical adjustments by opponents. The team's adaptability and depth were tested, but their ability to overcome these obstacles and secure vital points was a testament to their resilience and strategic planning.

Wrexham AFC's away performances in the 2024–25 season were a critical component of their successful promotion campaign. Through disciplined defensive strategies, efficient attacking play, and tactical adaptability, they established themselves as formidable opponents on the road. As they prepare for the challenges of the EFL Championship, maintaining and building upon this away form will be essential for continued success.

Preparing for the Championship   Tactical Strategies and Promotion Prospects

Wrexham AFC's ascent to the EFL Championship marks a significant milestone in the club's history. As they prepare for the challenges of the second tier, a comprehensive analysis of tactical strategies, squad development, and organizational planning is essential to ensure competitiveness and sustainability.

1. Tactical Evolution Under Phil Parkinson

Manager Phil Parkinson's pragmatic approach has been instrumental in Wrexham's recent successes. His emphasis on team cohesion, defensive solidity, and strategic adaptability has allowed the team to navigate the complexities of lower-tier football effectively. As Wrexham transitions to the Championship, Parkinson's experience and tactical acumen will be crucial in adapting to the higher level of competition. His focus on maintaining the club's culture and avoiding overreliance on star players aligns with the need for a balanced and resilient squad.

2. Squad Reinforcement and Transfer Strategy

Competing in the Championship requires a squad with depth, versatility, and experience. Wrexham's management is exploring the acquisition of seasoned professionals who can provide leadership and stability. Potential targets include veteran Premier League and Championship players capable of mentoring younger talents and contributing immediately on the pitch. The club's financial health, bolstered by increased revenues and global exposure, supports strategic investments in player acquisitions without compromising sustainability. However, careful consideration is necessary to balance wage structures and maintain team harmony.

3. Financial Management and Sustainability

Wrexham's financial strategy emphasizes long-term sustainability over short-term gains. The club's ownership has demonstrated a commitment to prudent spending, focusing on infrastructure development, youth academy enhancement, and community engagement. Revenue streams from global merchandise sales, sponsorships, and media rights, including the popular "Welcome to Wrexham" documentary, have strengthened the club's financial position. This approach ensures that investments in the playing squad and facilities are made responsibly, aligning with the club's values and long-term objectives.

4. Infrastructure and Facility Upgrades

To support the demands of Championship football, Wrexham is investing in infrastructure improvements, including the expansion of the Racecourse Ground and the enhancement of training facilities. These developments aim to provide players with state-of-the-art resources for preparation and recovery, while also accommodating a growing fanbase. Upgraded facilities contribute to player performance, injury prevention, and overall club appeal to potential recruits.

5. Youth Development and Academy Focus

Developing homegrown talent is a cornerstone of Wrexham's strategic plan. Investments in the youth academy aim to identify and nurture local prospects who can progress to the first team. This approach not only provides a sustainable pipeline of talent but also strengthens the club's connection with the community. Emphasizing youth development aligns with financial prudence and fosters a culture of loyalty and club identity.

6. Data Analytics and Performance Monitoring

Incorporating data analytics into player performance and match analysis is increasingly vital in modern football. Wrexham is adopting advanced metrics to assess player fitness, tactical effectiveness, and opposition tendencies. Utilizing technology for performance monitoring enables the coaching staff to make informed decisions regarding training regimens, match strategies, and player recruitment. This analytical approach enhances the club's competitive edge in the Championship.

7. Fan Engagement and Global Branding

Wrexham's rise has garnered international attention, expanding its fanbase beyond traditional boundaries. Engaging with supporters through social media, international tours, and merchandise has elevated the club's global profile. Maintaining this momentum requires consistent communication, community involvement, and brand development. A strong global presence not only boosts revenue but also attracts potential sponsors and partners, further solidifying the club's financial foundation.

8. Navigating Championship Competition

The Championship presents a diverse array of playing styles and tactical challenges. Wrexham must prepare to face teams with varying approaches, from possession-based systems to direct, physical play. Flexibility in tactics, in-game adaptability, and thorough opponent analysis will be essential. Building a squad capable of adjusting to different scenarios and maintaining consistency throughout the rigorous season is paramount for success.

9. Setting Realistic Objectives

While ambition drives progress, setting achievable goals is crucial in the Championship's competitive landscape. Prioritizing league survival, establishing a solid mid-table presence, and gradually building towards playoff contention allows for measured growth. This approach mitigates the risks associated with overextension and ensures that the club's development remains on a sustainable trajectory.

Wrexham AFC's transition to the Championship is a testament to strategic planning, effective management, and community support. By focusing on tactical adaptability, prudent financial practices, infrastructure development, and youth integration, the club is well-positioned to navigate the challenges of the second tier. Maintaining the club's identity and values will be instrumental in achieving long-term success and potentially realizing the dream of reaching the Premier League.

Wrexham AFC's Future Prospects and Long-Term Vision

Wrexham AFC's remarkable ascent—achieving three consecutive promotions to reach the EFL Championship—has captivated the football world. As the club prepares for the challenges of the second tier, its leadership is focused on sustainable growth, strategic investments, and a long-term vision that balances ambition with financial prudence.

1. Strategic Vision: From Championship Stability to Premier League Ambitions

Owners Ryan Reynolds and Rob McElhenney have transformed Wrexham into a globally recognized club. Their long-term objective is clear: establish Wrexham as a competitive force in the Championship with aspirations of reaching the Premier League. While co-owner McElhenney humorously claims unfamiliarity with the term "consolidation," the club acknowledges the need for measured progress, emphasizing sustainable development over rapid advancement.

2. Financial Strategy: Balancing Investment with Sustainability

Wrexham's financial health has improved significantly, with revenues reaching $55 million in 2024, bolstered by global merchandise sales, sponsorships, and media rights. Despite this growth, the club remains committed to financial responsibility, avoiding reckless spending in favor of strategic investments that ensure long-term stability.

3. Infrastructure Development: Enhancing Facilities for Future Success

To accommodate a growing fanbase and meet Championship standards, Wrexham is investing in infrastructure upgrades. Plans include the redevelopment of the Racecourse Ground, with a new 5,500-capacity Kop stand set to open in 2026. These enhancements aim to improve the matchday experience and provide state-of-the-art facilities for players and staff.

4. Global Expansion: Building an International Fanbase

The club's popularity has surged internationally, particularly in the United States, thanks to the "Welcome to Wrexham" docuseries and strategic marketing partnerships. Upcoming tours in Australia and New Zealand, along with matches against high-profile teams, are part of efforts to expand Wrexham's global footprint and attract new supporters.

5. Youth Development: Investing in Homegrown Talent

As Wrexham AFC continues to rise through the English football leagues, one of the key areas of focus for the club is the development of its youth academy. Co-owners **Ryan Reynolds** and **Rob McElhenney**, along with the coaching staff, recognize that building a sustainable pipeline of talent through youth development is crucial for long-term success. This strategic shift aims to not only produce homegrown stars for the first team but also to ensure that

Welcome to *Wrexham*: The Rise of the Red Dragons

Wrexham's future is underpinned by strong, self-sustaining foundations.

1. Academy Philosophy and Vision

At the heart of Wrexham's youth development strategy is a clear philosophy: to develop players who are not only technically proficient but also embody the values of the club. This includes a strong emphasis on discipline, hard work, and teamwork. The aim is to produce players who understand the culture of Wrexham and are ready to step into the first team when called upon.

Ryan Reynolds has expressed his long-term vision: "Building from the ground up, nurturing talent that represents the club's values, and making Wrexham a place where young players want to come and succeed." This philosophy aligns with the broader aim of making Wrexham a club that is sustainable both financially and in terms of its footballing achievements.

2. Investment in Youth Facilities

A significant aspect of this commitment to youth development is the investment in the club's **youth facilities**. In recent years, Wrexham has made considerable upgrades to their training infrastructure. The **Colliers Park Training Ground**, which houses the academy, has undergone enhancements to meet the increasing demands of youth development, with better pitches, gym facilities, and coaching resources.

The upgraded facilities allow the club to provide young players with the best possible environment to train and develop. This includes both **physical and mental conditioning**, ensuring that players are equipped for the rigors of professional football. The investment in infrastructure demonstrates the club's long-term commitment to developing homegrown talent that will eventually make an impact in the first team.

3. Scouting and Recruitment Strategy

Wrexham has been proactive in expanding its **scouting network** to identify young talent, both locally and nationally. The club's recruitment team works closely with local schools, academies, and regional football clubs to spot players who may not have had the opportunity to develop within the more established academies of larger clubs.

The scouting process at Wrexham is designed to be **holistic**: not only do scouts look for players with raw technical ability, but they also assess attributes like mental resilience, work ethic, and character. This is in line with the club's broader philosophy of focusing on team cohesion and maintaining a strong sense of unity and professionalism throughout the squad.

4. Player Development Pathway

Wrexham's youth academy has structured pathways that give young players the chance to progress into the senior squad. The club has established several age group teams ranging from **Under-9s** all the way to the **Under-18s**, with a clear progression route for the most promising players. Players are given the chance to train alongside the senior squad regularly, ensuring that they are familiar with the demands of the professional game.

The club's approach focuses on **individualized development plans** for each player, with the aim of identifying their strengths and areas for improvement. Players who show promise are given the opportunity to train with the first team, gaining invaluable experience before making the step up to professional football.

One example of this is **Elliot Lee,** who has progressed from youth academy product to senior player, featuring in a number of first-team matches. His journey through the academy system exemplifies the opportunities available to homegrown talent at Wrexham.

5. Collaboration with Local Communities

Wrexham's commitment to youth development goes beyond the football pitch. The club also aims to integrate its youth development efforts into the broader **community**, ensuring that young people in the area are given the chance to engage with the club and the sport. Wrexham AFC's outreach programs offer young people the chance to get involved in football, whether through coaching sessions, football camps, or other community initiatives.

This connection with local communities is crucial for developing a **talent pool** that is deeply embedded in the club's identity. By investing in grassroots football, Wrexham aims to foster a new generation of players who will continue to represent the club both on and off the pitch.

6. Long-Term Sustainability

One of the key aspects of Wrexham's youth development strategy is sustainability. By producing their own talent, the club can reduce its reliance on external signings, which in turn helps manage financial resources more efficiently. This self-sufficiency allows Wrexham to focus on **investing in players** who can be integrated into the team without having to spend large amounts on transfer fees.

Moreover, the development of homegrown talent is an essential component of the club's long-term strategy to **compete at higher levels**. As Wrexham progresses through the EFL Championship and, eventually, aims for the Premier League, having a strong youth academy will provide the club with the depth needed to compete at the highest levels without overreliance on external transfers.

7. Notable Young Players from the Academy

As part of Wrexham's investment in its youth system, several young players have begun to emerge as potential first-team prospects. Notable examples include:

- **Ethan Davidson** – A dynamic attacking midfielder who has impressed for the Under-18s. Davidson's vision and passing ability have drawn the attention of senior coaches, and he could soon make the leap to the senior squad.

- **Sam Hughes** – A promising center-back who has shown excellent defensive instincts and is considered a key player for the academy's future.

- **Lucas Barnes** – A talented winger with pace and technical ability, Barnes has been a standout player in the youth ranks and could provide valuable depth to the senior squad in the near future.

Wrexham AFC's commitment to **youth development** is a cornerstone of the club's long-term vision. By focusing on cultivating homegrown talent, investing in top-notch facilities, and expanding scouting efforts, Wrexham aims to establish a sustainable talent pipeline that can support the club's ambitions for years to come. The focus on community integration and individualized player development ensures that young talent is given the best chance to succeed, contributing to a future where Wrexham AFC not only competes at the highest levels but also remains grounded in the principles that have helped the club grow so rapidly under the leadership of **Ryan Reynolds** and **Rob McElhenney**.

6. Community Engagement: Strengthening Local Ties

Maintaining a strong connection with the local community remains a cornerstone of Wrexham's philosophy. Initiatives include community outreach programs, fan engagement activities, and partnerships with local organizations, ensuring that the club's growth benefits the wider Wrexham area.

7. Navigating Championship Challenges: Adapting to a Competitive Landscape

The Championship presents a highly competitive environment with diverse playing styles and tactical approaches. Wrexham plans to adapt by enhancing its scouting network, investing in player development, and employing data analytics to inform strategic decisions. Manager Phil Parkinson's experience and adaptability will be crucial in guiding the team through this transition.

8. A Vision Rooted in Ambition and Sustainability

Wrexham AFC's journey from the National League to the Championship is a testament to strategic planning, community support, and visionary leadership. As the club looks to the future, its focus on sustainable growth, infrastructure development, and global expansion positions it well to achieve its long-term goals, including the ultimate ambition of reaching the Premier League.

PART II

Phil Parkinson

The Call to North Wales

It began with a phone call—one that would change the course of a historic club and reshape the legacy of a seasoned football manager.

Phil Parkinson was no stranger to the grind of English football. With a managerial career that had taken him from Colchester to Bradford City, Bolton Wanderers to Sunderland, he had earned a reputation for resilience, discipline, and methodical leadership. His teams weren't always flashy, but they were always prepared— difficult to beat, deeply bonded, and quietly ambitious. But when Wrexham AFC came calling in the summer of 2021, it was something different. Something unexpected.

Wrexham was, at that point, a sleeping giant—one of the oldest football clubs in the world, rich with history but stuck in the National League for over a decade. The club had faded into the lower tiers of English football, far from the bright lights and top-flight glory. Yet hope stirred again when actors Ryan Reynolds and Rob McElhenney purchased the club in a headline-grabbing takeover. Their vision was bold: to restore Wrexham to its rightful place in English football—and beyond.

The media frenzy surrounding the ownership was immediate and intense, but the club still needed something more crucial than Hollywood attention: a leader who could turn fantasy into footballing reality.

Enter Phil Parkinson.

At first glance, he didn't fit the celebrity narrative. He wasn't flamboyant. He didn't come with viral moments or movie-star charisma. But what he brought was far more valuable—a steady hand, years of tactical know-how, and a belief in team-first football. His appointment marked a clear signal: Wrexham wasn't just aiming to make headlines—they were aiming to win.

Welcome to *Wrexham*: The Rise of the Red Dragons

The offer came with a challenge Parkinson couldn't ignore. Here was a club with potential, with resources, and now with a global spotlight. But it also came with expectations most National League managers would never face. "Why Phil Parkinson?" some questioned. But those who knew the game understood: he was a builder, not just a manager.

Phil arrived in North Wales quietly, almost in contrast to the noise surrounding the club. His first impressions of Wrexham were of pride and hunger. The town had been bruised by years of sporting disappointment, but its soul remained intact. The fans still packed the Racecourse Ground with unwavering loyalty. They didn't just want results—they craved restoration.

The challenge was immense. The club needed rebuilding from the ground up: recruiting the right players, instilling a winning culture, managing newfound fame, and turning a media story into a football story. Parkinson's early months were consumed with scouting, restructuring, and redefining what it meant to wear the Wrexham badge.

What set Parkinson apart from other coaches wasn't just his tactical intelligence—it was his ability to read people. He knew which players needed tough love and which ones needed quiet reassurance. He demanded commitment but gave clarity. Training under him was precise and intense, with one goal: improvement every day.

Behind the scenes, the new ownership backed him with full confidence. Ryan and Rob made their support clear, not just through resources, but through trust. They gave Parkinson autonomy, recognizing that their dream required real football minds to build the foundation.

His first season wasn't without challenges. Every draw felt like a disaster in the eyes of the media. Every mistake was magnified by the cameras rolling for the documentary. But Parkinson remained composed. He never let the noise rattle him. "We win by focusing on the football," he often told his players.

By the end of that first year, Wrexham had found more than just form—they had found belief. The system was clicking. The players were united. The club felt alive again.

Phil Parkinson didn't come to Wrexham to be a star in someone else's story. He came to build something real—and in doing so, he quietly began writing one of the most remarkable chapters in modern football.

Building the Foundation

Success in football rarely arrives by accident. It's not born of hype or headlines, but of the quiet, deliberate work done behind closed doors—on the training pitch, in the dressing room, and in the minds of players who come to believe in something greater than themselves. That's where Phil Parkinson began.

His first few months at Wrexham were not defined by press conferences or grand declarations. They were defined by structure— by laying a foundation not only for a team, but for a culture. Parkinson understood that if Wrexham were to rise, they needed more than tactics. They needed identity.

From day one, Parkinson set out to answer one question: *What does it mean to play for Wrexham?*

He knew that the club's history was vast, stretching back to 1864, but history alone couldn't win matches. The players needed to feel connected to something tangible—something they could carry into every tackle, every run, every decision on the field.

Training sessions under Parkinson were intense but purposeful. Everything had a rhythm—defensive shape, transitions, movement off the ball. He brought clarity to a squad that had previously lacked direction. More than that, he reintroduced standards. Players were expected to be early, to train hard, and to leave everything on the pitch. "Preparation equals performance," he reminded them constantly.

His recruitment strategy was surgical. Rather than chasing big names, Parkinson focused on balance—finding players not only with skill but with character. He brought in leaders, workers, thinkers. Some came with experience in higher leagues, others with hunger from lower ones. What they all shared was a willingness to buy into a shared vision.

Among his earliest key signings was Paul Mullin, a striker with a relentless engine and a nose for goal. Mullin had just been named League Two's Player of the Season, and signing him was a bold statement. Here was a League Two star choosing to drop a division for a National League side. Why? Because he believed in the project. Because Parkinson had made him believe.

Inside the dressing room, trust was building. Parkinson was not a screamer. He didn't rant and rave. Instead, he pulled players aside, challenged them to be better, and gave them ownership of their roles. He built a culture where accountability was not about fear—it was about pride.

Off the pitch, the club was evolving too. With Ryan and Rob investing in facilities, media, and fan engagement, Wrexham was becoming a model of modern football culture. But Parkinson kept the team grounded. "Ignore the cameras," he'd say. "Focus on what we can control."

There were bumps along the way. A frustrating draw here, a missed opportunity there. Critics questioned whether the plan was too ambitious. But Parkinson never blinked. He knew what he was building wasn't temporary. He wasn't chasing a single promotion—he was creating a system for sustained success.

Gradually, the results followed. Wrexham became harder to break down, smarter in possession, and more clinical in attack. The players began to gel, not just as professionals, but as a unit. There was joy in the work, pride in the badge, and fire in their performances.

The turning point that season wasn't just a win—it was a mindset shift. After a gritty comeback victory against a top-of-the-table rival, Parkinson gathered the team in the dressing room and said, "That's what belief looks like. That's what we are."

The media began to take notice. The Racecourse Ground buzzed with excitement. Fans who had grown used to disappointment were now daring to hope. Parkinson remained calm, never letting early success breed complacency. "We haven't achieved anything yet," he'd remind the squad. "This is just the groundwork."

He wasn't wrong. The season was still long, the league still ruthless. But something had changed—something deeper than results. Wrexham were no longer chasing momentum. They were creating it.

And at the center of it all was Phil Parkinson—building patiently, building deliberately, building for something far greater than just promotion.

He was building a belief that Wrexham was coming back.

A Town Awakens

Wrexham is more than just a football club. It's the heartbeat of a proud community—brick by brick, voice by voice, history in every street. For decades, the club had been both a source of identity and a mirror of the town's struggles. When fortunes declined on the pitch, something dimmed in the soul of the town too.

But in Phil Parkinson's first full season, something began to stir. The chants grew louder. The crowds swelled. Hope, that most fragile of emotions, returned—and this time, it was being carefully guarded by a man who understood its power.

To understand what Parkinson achieved in those early months, one must understand Wrexham's unique bond with its team. Unlike many modern clubs, Wrexham hadn't lost its roots. Fans didn't come for spectacle—they came for belonging. They came because the red and white wasn't just colour; it was family, memory, and pride. And Parkinson didn't just respect that—he nurtured it.

At community events, the players now showed up—not as distant stars, but as neighbours. The gaffer made it clear: you don't just play for Wrexham, *you represent Wrexham*. His team walked the local streets, visited schools, supported causes. They weren't above the town—they were of it.

Matchdays at the Racecourse Ground became rituals again. Families came early, supporters filled pubs and alleys with songs, and the stadium pulsed with a defiance that hadn't been felt in years. For Parkinson, this wasn't just atmosphere—it was fuel.

His players fed off the energy. Paul Mullin, now firmly the club's talisman, found a level of form that made headlines weekly. His goals were precise, passionate, and often decisive. But it wasn't just Mullin—Ollie Palmer, Ben Tozer, Jordan Davies, and a growing group of standouts made the pitch feel alive. The team wasn't just winning; they were thrilling.

Behind the touchline, Parkinson remained steady. While fans erupted in the stands, he stood focused, rarely gesturing wildly. His authority came not from volume, but from clarity. He managed the chaos with calm. When the team surged, he cooled them. When they struggled, he anchored them.

It wasn't all smooth sailing. There were moments when doubt crept back in—last-minute goals conceded, a harsh red card, a defensive lapse at a crucial juncture. But this time, the team responded. There was no unraveling. They bounced back stronger, tougher, more united. Parkinson's resilience had become their resilience.

Outside of football, the town of Wrexham began to transform. Businesses flourished with the influx of visitors, documentaries showcased its charm to a global audience, and the people held their heads a little higher. A story was unfolding—and Wrexham wasn't just the setting, it was the protagonist.

One local supporter, an elderly man who had attended matches since the 1950s, put it best:
"We've had managers before who brought tactics. But Parkinson brought belief—quietly, patiently, like he knew it was always ours, just waiting to be woken."

The Disney+ documentary cameras captured the goals, the fans, the drama—but what they couldn't always capture was the deeper shift. In the streets, in the pubs, in the schools and the homes—Wrexham was rising. And at the center of that rise was a man who never sought the spotlight but knew how to build something worth watching.

Phil Parkinson didn't transform Wrexham with one moment. He did it with many—training ground drills, quiet chats in corridors, halftime talks that reset the tone, and above all, an unwavering belief in what could be.

By the season's midpoint, one thing was certain: this wasn't just a football campaign. This was a reawakening.

Wrexham had found its voice again.

And the town was singing in harmony with its team.

The First Breakthrough

Every long journey is marked by moments—those hard-won victories that shift a season's narrative from hope to certainty. For Phil Parkinson and Wrexham, the first real breakthrough didn't come with fanfare, but with grit. It was less a turning point than a statement: *We are no longer just contenders. We are ready.*

By early spring, the league table had begun to tighten. Wrexham, once quietly climbing, was now in the thick of a title race. The margins were fine—one point here, a clean sheet there—but the focus had never been sharper.

Parkinson, a veteran of football's unpredictable trenches, kept his squad grounded. "Let the fans dream," he told the players. "Our job is to work." While the town buzzed with promotion fever, Parkinson returned to fundamentals: fitness, focus, and finishing.

It was during this crucial stretch that a key fixture arrived—an away match against a fierce title rival. The kind of game that defines character, not just form. The pressure was immense. The cameras were rolling. The stakes were high.

Wrexham went down early.

For a lesser side, it could've spelled disaster. For Parkinson's men, it was a challenge. The response was instant—not from panic, but from principle. Every man on the pitch stuck to the plan. They passed with purpose, defended with discipline, and waited for the cracks to appear.

Midway through the second half, the reward came. A thundering header from a set-piece—a move rehearsed again and again in training. Level. Then, ten minutes from time, Paul Mullin latched onto a through-ball and calmly slotted it past the keeper.

Welcome to *Wrexham*: The Rise of the Red Dragons

Wrexham had turned the match on its head.

The final whistle triggered a storm of celebration, both in the away end and back home in pubs and living rooms across North Wales. But Parkinson didn't punch the air. He simply nodded, turned, and led his team off the pitch. This was business.

That victory wasn't just about three points. It was a message: Wrexham could beat the best, under pressure, away from home. It galvanized belief within the squad and signaled to the rest of the league that this team wasn't fading. It was rising.

From that day forward, performances sharpened. The midfield became tighter, the defence more commanding, and the attack increasingly ruthless. Parkinson rotated wisely, ensuring legs stayed fresh and minds stayed alert. His man-management shone—not every player could start, but every player felt seen.

Behind closed doors, Parkinson's leadership became even more evident. After each match, win or lose, he conducted debriefs not to point fingers, but to build understanding. He'd replay clips, ask players what they saw, and invite reflection. This wasn't a dictatorship—it was a learning culture.

He also remained a master of momentum. When the team strung together three wins in a row, he reminded them, "Consistency is earned, not given." When they drew a game they should have won, he called it a "lesson, not a loss."

Fans started to travel in larger numbers. The Racecourse Ground became a fortress. Visiting teams began arriving knowing they would have to fight for every inch. The red shirts no longer carried weight just from history—they carried form, force, and fearlessness.

And still, Parkinson refused to look ahead. "One game at a time," he said again and again to reporters. But inside the dressing room, he added one more line: *"Let's make people remember us."*

The breakthrough wasn't just about results. It was about identity. Wrexham had become a team with a clear spine: strong in character, bold in attack, resilient in adversity. A team that reflected the best parts of the man who led them.

As the final stretch of the season loomed, one thing was undeniable: Wrexham had become more than a story.

They had become a force.

And Parkinson had become more than a manager.

He was the architect of a rising legend.

Trials and Turning Points

No great story ever unfolds without adversity. And for Phil Parkinson's Wrexham, the road to glory was anything but smooth. The higher the climb, the fiercer the winds. Every winning streak was shadowed by mounting expectations. Every missed opportunity was dissected in full view. And every setback—on or off the pitch—demanded the strength of a leader who refused to flinch.

The spring months brought a fresh wave of pressure. Injuries began to test squad depth. Key players picked up knocks—some minor, others more serious. Opponents, increasingly aware of Wrexham's threat, adjusted their tactics, often resorting to physical play or deep defensive lines. Matches turned gritty. Victories became narrower. A sense of tension returned.

For the first time in weeks, Wrexham stumbled. A frustrating draw at home. A shock defeat away. Questions surfaced in the media. Was the momentum slipping? Could Parkinson adapt?

But adversity had always been his teacher—and his ally.

Rather than panic, Parkinson recalibrated. He rotated his lineup with precision, gave fringe players meaningful chances, and restored the psychological edge that had momentarily dulled. Team meetings shifted focus from pressure to purpose. "We've come too far to blink," he told them. "Now's the time to lean in."

And lean in they did.

One particular turning point came during a tense home fixture against a mid-table side. The atmosphere that night at the Racecourse was different—not electric, but anxious. Fans sensed the importance. It wasn't just about winning—it was about reclaiming rhythm.

The game was tight. The opposition defended deep, time-wasted, and frustrated. Wrexham couldn't break through. As the clock ticked past 85 minutes, some supporters had begun to accept a goalless draw.

Then, a spark.

A quick one-two down the right. A lofted cross. And a towering header from the captain—thundering into the net. The roar was deafening. Not just a celebration, but a release.

Wrexham had found their pulse again.

Phil Parkinson didn't celebrate wildly. He looked to the bench, fist clenched, and gave a single nod. That moment wasn't luck—it was resilience. Built in training, forged in discipline, and executed under fire.

Off the pitch, other challenges tested Parkinson's leadership. The growing fame of the club—fueled by the global reach of the documentary and the celebrity ownership—brought new distractions. Media appearances. International interest. External noise. But Parkinson remained unmoved.

He kept his players focused on the basics—tactics, teamwork, and community connection. He reminded them constantly that fame was fleeting, but legacy lasted. "People are watching," he told them, "but more importantly, people are believing. Let's not let them down."

In press conferences, he was courteous but curt. Never distracted by headlines. Never feeding hype. His job was not to entertain—it was to deliver.

Back in the dressing room, he doubled down on unity. Senior players were given more responsibility, younger players mentored, and even those not in the matchday squad were made to feel essential. Parkinson knew that championships weren't won by a starting eleven—they were won by a squad.

And in Wrexham's darkest hours of the campaign, that squad stood tall.

By the end of April, the storm had passed. Wrexham were back at the summit—or within striking distance. The fans, tested and true, had never wavered. Their belief was not born of recent victories—it was born of a shared journey. A journey now etched in trials, but also in triumph.

For Phil Parkinson, these challenges were not detours. They were necessary chapters. The making of a team that knew how to win—but also how to fight, how to fall, and most importantly, how to rise.

With just weeks to go, one truth rang out across the town, the terraces, and the training ground:

Wrexham was ready.

The Final Push

The end of a season is unlike any other part of the campaign. It's not just about form or tactics—it's about heart, nerve, and a refusal to blink when the world is watching. For Phil Parkinson and his Wrexham squad, the final stretch became a cauldron of pressure and purpose. Each fixture felt heavier. Each point was precious. Every breath the town took seemed to echo with one question: *Is this our time?*

The run-in was brutal. No gifts, no easy games, and no margin for error. The league table had crystallized into a two-horse race. A single slip could end it all.

But Parkinson had prepared for this long before April. Every preseason drill, every halftime talk, every rotated squad—it had all led to this. Wrexham, under his steady guidance, didn't just enter the final push—they charged into it.

One of the defining moments came at home—a match circled on every calendar, against a fierce promotion rival. The kind of game legends are born in. The Racecourse Ground was a sea of red, alive with belief and bursting with tension. Fans arrived hours early. The players walked onto the pitch to a wall of sound that shook the stadium to its bones.

Parkinson's team started with fire. Aggression in the press. Precision in the pass. But the opposition were no passengers—they hit back hard. The first half ended level, nerves fraying on both sides.

At halftime, Parkinson didn't scream. He steadied.

"You've worked for this moment," he told them. "Trust the work. Trust each other."

What followed was not just a performance—it was a statement. Wrexham poured forward with courage. The breakthrough came from a sweeping move finished with grace. Then another—this time from a substitute Parkinson had introduced just moments earlier. Tactical genius wrapped in humility.

The final whistle sparked scenes of sheer ecstasy. Fans wept. Players embraced. Parkinson, as ever, stood just a few steps back, soaking it in quietly.

The media tried to pry a reaction—*Are you confident? Is this the year?* He smiled, always the pragmatist. "There's work still to do. Nothing's won yet."

But inside the club, a different energy had taken hold. The dressing room felt like family. The training ground buzzed with intent. Even off the pitch, local businesses and fans could feel the pull of destiny.

Phil Parkinson didn't allow complacency to creep in. He pushed harder in those final weeks than ever before. Recovery sessions were intensified. Analysis became sharper. Mindset training was introduced, ensuring players were not only physically ready—but mentally indomitable.

When Wrexham travelled away for their final two fixtures, the scenes were surreal. Thousands followed. Roads into small towns were clogged with red-and-white scarves. It felt less like a football match and more like a pilgrimage.

And yet, Parkinson kept things normal. Familiar routines. Simple meals. Quiet walkthroughs. He didn't want his players chasing history—he wanted them chasing the next ball.

By the time the final whistle of the final game sounded—with Wrexham victorious and their place in the history books secured—Phil Parkinson allowed himself something rare: a visible smile. A long, proud, unfiltered moment.

He embraced his coaching staff, hugged his players, and walked across the pitch to the away fans, hands raised not in self-congratulation, but in gratitude.

It was done.

Wrexham had earned promotion. And they had done it Parkinson's way—through resolve, respect, and relentless consistency.

The final push had tested everything. But it also revealed everything—the strength of the system, the steel of the players, and the soul of a leader who never let the dream overtake the discipline.

As the players lifted the trophy, and the Racecourse exploded in celebration days later, Parkinson stepped back once again.

He knew the story was far from over.

But this chapter—this magnificent, magical, meteoric chapter—belonged to Wrexham.

And to the man who never blinked.

Beyond Promotion – Building for the Future

The champagne had barely dried on the Racecourse turf when Phil Parkinson's mind turned to the next challenge. For others, promotion was a finish line. For him, it was merely the end of one race—and the starting gun for another.

The new chapter Wrexham had earned came with new terrain: tougher opponents, higher stakes, faster football. The cameras, still rolling from the Hollywood-backed documentary, loved the fairy tale. But Parkinson knew fairy tales end unless you write the next one with equal intensity.

His first move? Stability. Success can unravel quickly without it. He worked closely with the board, not just on transfers, but on infrastructure. Improvements to the training ground. Expanded analytics. Recruitment staff with League experience. Parkinson wasn't just managing a squad—he was sculpting a sustainable future.

Still, he never lost his connection to the soul of the club. He made time for staff who had been there long before him. The kit man. The groundskeepers. The lifelong supporters who now saw their town on the global stage. For Parkinson, their pride mattered as much as any title.

Player retention became the next battle. Some feared bigger clubs would poach Wrexham's stars. But Parkinson didn't beg players to stay—he gave them reasons to. His loyalty, his vision, and his honesty spoke louder than contracts.

"I won't promise comfort," he told one key player. "But I'll promise a fight worth showing up for every week."

The off-season buzzed with recruitment. Not just for talent, but for character. Parkinson had no room for egos. He sought players who fit the culture, who would bleed for the badge, who understood that the climb was far from over.

Pre-season began with a sharpened tone. Fitness demands increased. Tactical drills intensified. The coaching staff, molded in Parkinson's image, left no detail untouched. If the club was to survive and thrive in the next division, it had to evolve—quickly.

Meanwhile, the global spotlight grew brighter. Wrexham wasn't just a club now—it was a symbol. A working-class town reborn. A football team that proved grit and glory could coexist. And Phil Parkinson was at the center of it all, not basking in fame, but guiding it wisely.

He allowed the documentary cameras in, but on his terms. They could film the passion, not the plan. They could celebrate the noise, but not at the cost of focus. He protected his players from distraction, always anchoring them to the mission.

And the mission was simple: to prove they belonged.

Welcome to *Wrexham*: The Rise of the Red Dragons

The new season kicked off with a roar. Wrexham, fearless and unified, took to the higher division not as tourists, but as contenders. The football was sharper. The decisions faster. Mistakes punished more ruthlessly. Yet Parkinson's team met the moment with maturity.

There were early wins, hard-fought draws, and a few humbling losses. But the foundations held. And in every press conference, Parkinson struck the same tone: measured, forward-thinking, respectful of the journey but never sentimental.

One reporter asked him, "Is the goal now to survive or to succeed?"

His reply was classic Parkinson: "We survived the hard years. Now we build."

Behind the scenes, he nurtured the youth system, wanting local talent to rise. He attended U18 matches. He mentored academy coaches. If Wrexham's story was going to last, it had to be rooted in the next generation.

And through it all, the fans never stopped singing. Not just for the players—but for the man who brought belief back to the terraces. Phil Parkinson, their steady hand. Their silent general.

Because while the world saw a club reborn, the people of Wrexham knew: their rise wasn't accidental. It was built brick by brick, moment by moment, under the guidance of a man who never craved headlines—only results.

The journey wasn't over. In many ways, it had just begun.

But thanks to Parkinson, Wrexham wasn't just dreaming anymore.

They were planning.

The Hollywood Effect – Fame, Football, and Staying Grounded

Wrexham was once a name whispered in local pubs and printed in lower-league matchday programmes. But now, thanks to the high-profile ownership of Ryan Reynolds and Rob McElhenney, it echoed across continents. American fans wore red. Netflix subscribers cheered for a club they'd never heard of two years prior. Suddenly, Wrexham wasn't just a team—it was a global sensation.

For Phil Parkinson, the arrival of fame presented both opportunity and challenge. His players were now recognisable on both sides of the Atlantic. Airport selfies became common. Media days doubled. Social media buzzed with every touch, tackle, and tweet.

But Parkinson never let the dressing room drift into a movie script. He respected the new chapter, welcomed the attention—it helped the club grow—but he made it clear: the glitz wasn't the game.

"I told the lads, the cameras can't score goals," he recalled. "You still have to earn every result on the pitch."

Reynolds and McElhenney, to their credit, respected that vision. They weren't in it for ego or vanity. They trusted Parkinson, empowering him to run the football side without interference. What they brought was infrastructure, ambition, and a storytelling megaphone the size of Hollywood.

And Parkinson used it wisely.

With investment came upgrades—modern facilities, improved nutrition plans, and stronger scouting networks. More staff were brought in, many handpicked by Parkinson for their integrity and expertise. Players now had access to resources once reserved for top-flight clubs. But beneath the shine, Parkinson ensured the values remained intact: humility, hard work, and unity.

Meanwhile, the cameras rolled. The docuseries *Welcome to Wrexham* didn't just show matches—it showed moments. Moments of heartbreak in the dressing room. Parkinson's quiet encouragement before a vital away fixture. A team meeting where tactics met tension. The human side of football.

And in these moments, the world saw Parkinson's genius—not as a showman, but as a steward. A man who steadied the ship when fame threatened to tip it.

He was never distracted. Fame didn't make the opponent weaker. It didn't guarantee three points. If anything, it raised expectations. And that meant higher stakes for every game, more pressure on every player, and less margin for error.

So he doubled down on discipline. Social media rules. Media training. Mental health support. He built not just better players—but stronger people. His approach was holistic, and his players responded.

Even as Hollywood royalty attended games, Parkinson treated it as background noise. At the Racecourse Ground, the only stars that mattered were the ones fighting for the badge.

Still, Parkinson recognised the good the fame brought. More fans. More revenue. More joy for the community. Local businesses thrived. Young children wore Wrexham shirts in places where Premier League kits once dominated. The town glowed with pride.

And Parkinson never took that lightly. In every community event he attended—school visits, charity fundraisers, supporters' dinners—he carried the weight of that pride with grace. He wasn't just a manager anymore. He was a symbol of the town's revival.

His players followed suit. Fame didn't fracture the squad—it bonded them. They became ambassadors of the club, shaped by Parkinson's quiet example.

Of course, the cameras occasionally caught tough moments too. Dressing room frustrations. Post-match heartbreaks. Tactical debates. But Parkinson never sought to curate his image. He just told the truth, did the work, and trusted that authenticity would speak louder than any script.

And it did.

Across the world, fans praised not just the fairytale of Wrexham— but the grounded, disciplined leadership behind it. The man who stood in the storm and pointed true north.

Phil Parkinson didn't chase Hollywood. It came to him.

And he met it with boots on the ground, eyes on the ball, and a heart full of purpose.

Setbacks and Second Winds – The Cost of Progress

Football, like life, doesn't move in a straight line.

For every rise, there's resistance. For every roaring crowd, there's a moment of stunned silence. And even with momentum, fame, and a revitalised club, Wrexham—under Phil Parkinson—had to face what every ambitious team eventually does: the hard reality of growing pains.

The step up in league brought new adversaries. Opponents with sharper tactics, deeper benches, and years of experience at that level. Parkinson's men were no longer underdogs; they were a known force—studied, targeted, and tested.

Injury setbacks began to pile up early in the season. Key players missed matches. The rhythm faltered. Parkinson had to dig deep into the squad, rotating players, testing formations, and trusting his depth. But depth, while improved, still struggled under the weight of expectation.

Wrexham went through a run of poor results. Fans grew anxious. The press poked at tactics. Critics questioned whether the Hollywood-fueled story had finally hit its ceiling.

But Parkinson was unmoved.

In post-match interviews, his voice never wavered. "We didn't come here for comfort," he'd say. "We came here to earn everything." Behind the scenes, he remained tireless—re-watching footage late into the night, talking one-on-one with players, refining strategies with his staff.

He reminded his squad that setbacks were part of the journey. That growth demands discomfort. And that trust—between player and coach, between fan and team—was forged not just in triumph, but in turbulence.

Still, there were moments that tested him personally.

A cup exit to a lower-league team. A last-minute goal conceded after 89 minutes of domination. A chorus of doubt from outside the town, questioning whether Parkinson's methods were outdated in a fast-evolving game.

But those closest to him—his coaching team, the players, and even the club's owners—never wavered in their belief. Ryan Reynolds and Rob McElhenney stood behind him, praising not just his results but his resilience. They saw the bigger picture: Parkinson had built more than a team. He had built a culture.

Mid-season became a period of recalibration. Parkinson adjusted training intensity to reduce injuries. He gave starts to younger players hungry to prove themselves. He held closed-door sessions focused on mentality—how to endure, adapt, and reemerge stronger.

And then came a turning point.

A gritty away win against a top-of-the-table side. It wasn't flashy, but it was full of fight. The players ran themselves into the ground. The bench roared every clearance. The fans sang louder than they had in weeks.

That night, Parkinson walked off the pitch with no fist-pumps or theatrics. Just a nod to the traveling supporters and a quiet conversation with his assistant. But inside, he knew: the second wind had arrived.

Wrexham began to climb again—slowly, purposefully. The style wasn't always pretty, but the results returned. Players grew wiser. The team became more tactically flexible, more emotionally resilient. And Parkinson, ever the architect, adjusted each piece with the care of a craftsman.

The setbacks, it turned out, were gifts in disguise. They forged a harder edge, a stronger spine. They reminded everyone involved that the road to lasting success is never without struggle.

And most importantly, they deepened the bond between the town and their team.

Because when Wrexham stumbled, it didn't fall apart. It pulled together. Fans packed the stands even tighter. Local businesses doubled down on their support. And in the heart of it all stood Phil Parkinson—weathered, wise, and unwavering.

Setbacks didn't scare him. They revealed him.

And with every storm faced, Wrexham grew closer to becoming not just a good team—but a great club.

Legacy in Motion – The Man Behind the Miracle

As the seasons passed and Wrexham continued its remarkable ascent, the conversation inevitably turned to legacy. What would be remembered of this era—not just the scores, the standings, or the silverware—but the spirit behind the revival?

At the center of it all stood Phil Parkinson.

He was never the loudest voice in the room, nor the flashiest name in the headlines. But ask anyone who played under him, worked beside him, or simply watched from the Racecourse Ground's packed terraces, and they'd agree: Parkinson had become the soul of the modern Wrexham story.

Legacy, for Parkinson, wasn't about statues or speeches. It was about foundations. The kind of legacy you build quietly—in training sessions on cold mornings, in tough team talks after narrow defeats, in the belief you instill in players who once doubted themselves.

He didn't just bring Wrexham back to relevance—he brought them back to life.

The club's transformation under his leadership wasn't just about tactics or transfers. It was cultural. He resurrected professionalism without sacrificing passion. He balanced ambition with humility. He proved that even in a football landscape increasingly dominated by quick fixes and big money, a clear vision and consistent leadership still mattered.

And the results spoke for themselves.

Promotion was no longer a dream—it was a step achieved. The club once languishing in non-league obscurity now held its own among seasoned professionals. Infrastructure improved. Academy talent emerged. Wrexham became a destination—not a detour.

Yet Parkinson never claimed the spotlight.

He often deflected praise to his staff, his players, or the unwavering fans. But everyone knew who laid the bricks. From the moment he walked through the door, he had given Wrexham something it desperately needed: belief.

Ryan Reynolds and Rob McElhenney, who once hoped only to save a club, now found themselves at the helm of a movement. And in interviews, they rarely finished a sentence about the team's success without crediting "Phil."

Supporters saw it, too. Chants of "There's only one Phil Parkinson" echoed louder with each season. His name became etched in the town's fabric—not as a celebrity, but as one of their own.

And yet, Parkinson never stopped working. Never grew complacent. He often reminded his team—and himself—that success was a moving target. "We haven't reached the ceiling," he'd say. "This is still a work in progress."

Perhaps that's what defined his legacy most: the refusal to settle.

Even as Wrexham's story captured hearts around the world, Parkinson kept building—not for cameras or headlines, but for the town, the badge, and the future.

In the end, legacy wasn't a final destination for Phil Parkinson.

It was momentum.

A steady heartbeat that would echo long after his time on the touchline. A culture of excellence rooted in resilience. A club reborn, not through miracles, but through method, sweat, and steady hands.

As the sun set on another successful season and the chants rang out through the Racecourse once again, Phil Parkinson looked on—not as a man chasing legacy, but as a man who had quietly become one.

150

Manufactured by Amazon.ca
Acheson, AB

31863411R00083